THE LAST/LOST EPIC

Iván Argüelles

Cyberwit.net
HIG 45 Kaushambi Kunj, Kalindipuram
Allahabad - 211011 (U.P.) India
http://www.cyberwit.net
Tel: +(91) 9415091004 +(91) (532) 2552257
E-mail: info@cyberwit.net

Printed at Repro India Limited.

i

the beginning is the end the alpha
erased and not re-created the vexing
night troubled sequences of memory
interrupted by red and the planet it
represents nostalgia in small wafers
eyes shut in communion with a deity
stone and wax and mortality poised
on the tip of an invisible spear
the language of bees in sleep the one
and misunderstanding which comes
with breathing and always the question
for why were we born only to suffer ?
what grass is and the infernal
quotation buried somewhere in the lawn
the cuttings taken tenderly and pasted
wasn't he a "darling" our Achilles
and the sea-girt rocks mourning like
mothers whom a god inspires to *know*
what is to the left of fate's wheel
turning in the garage of its own accord
whetstone and alcohol side by side
and behind in the small morass
of weed clumps and discarded glass
the rickety fence meant to keep winter
out for another day at least the air
brittle turning grey-white lonesome
as the eyes of Athena on her parapet
owl-shape and stumped as to the oracle
its deliberately twisted syllables a pyre
of vowels and utterances raving mad

a prediction no sooner emitted than
smoke and clouds that gather in knots
and the enormous boom of thunder
in the grape-yard as if rolling barrels
across the firmament of destruction
the massive units of unkempt matter
voluble entities razed in a minute
by a fiery epistle as an introduction
a proemium a forward to the last epic
that is being inscribed on a surface
the size of a thumbnail the reverse of
any given script the totality of ideograms
picture book recollections of ink as
it spreads its history over the page
and the page itself the denial of time
a river flooding over exegetical blanks
what I never meant to say but did
so anyway in a confession of grief
doubled down for the count to infinity
knees and shoulders of human emotion
depths of discontinuous language *the*
and *the* again dot dot dot of coding
frills and vagaries of sunlight interred
in the famous concrete slabs of knowledge
inarticulate as the beta that goes lost
with fingers and ivy and twilight
the color of time in the hills west of
this dislocation where again an effort
to resound echoes its yearning syllable
in a string of lunations and sorrowing
here place the palm down on the wet
and listen if possible to the remote
unwinding its tresses in the emblem

reflections of the irreversible
the unending yet unknown of silence
the backside the sheer edge of space
drop off to sleep still talking to
the *other* the only and gone

ii

and if there is no beginning only middle
the center everywhere and nothing holds
to one side or the other ellipse and eclipse
falling the fell motion of dying before birth
and what of the death after death and the
saga of light in graded shades and who interfere
and who dispel clouds and the yawning abyss
the four and the five that have no three or six
what does not follow cannot proceed from
and to wake from the unremembered dream
interuterine strife already with the *other*
eyes opened for the first and last time
and what is that wailing in the walls and what
the infirmity underfoot and the lassitude and
corruption of the elements and air and earth
fire and water the heraclitean flux cannot number
which is the next in the series of rotating sounds
we call language the tumbrel and thimble full
of vowels shaken for the lottery of thought
and will you be mine tonight you will you teach
me the dance the great round one of Krishna ?
and if the origins are beyond the pale of imagination
and only the kaleidoscope and vertigo are lessons
and the thumb orients the mouth and the tongue
pronounces sleeping the dithyramb and echo
and all run afoul of the lamp and the door and
what goes on behind the locked one faint
murmurings the Parcae with thread and scissors
and a fork to tune the melody and the tortoise shell
where they are playing at knuckle-bones the gods

come into being by the merest thunderclap
full born and gorgeously shining shadowless
radiating fulminant and enigmatic proportions
and if all is central to all everything runs off
the edge and the margins disappear in ink
and we are talking at one another full noon
hand to hand combat with speech the oracular
and it is all *medias res* the storm-driven ships
flailing in the Middle Sea in a perfect Latin
of scansioned hexameter and sybilline accent
where in the middle is the end ? bewail they
the castoffs of Troy and sea is everywhere
at one with cloud and abyss spectral lands
of night and the key and the clue to Underground
reciting prayers and myths and summoning
viscera translucent as flares to read darkening
the eternal fate of and et cetera arms akimbo
like statues learning to stride the mountains
dimly remembering and faltering in their Doric
sparring with satellites and peripheral moons
monkey and dragon and elephant the Heights !
and if after the ending things regroup themselves
isolated spaces fill in a rush of promontories
with cliffs and vergers and legends and Nymphs
it all comes around the eternal return of time
the every which way of seeing and not seeing
mind in its precipitous cavity veering off
nothing holds and leaf and finger shudder
smoke reduces the sky sailors seizing whatever
floats in the disarray of water and endlessness

iii

the gods those pluperfect entities
star-spun and star-spent is there ever
a last time for them or do they exist
only in the *idea* of their perfected selves
and if they do have memory does it
extend back to the infinity before time
or do they remember nothing except
what happened the day before yesterday
do they exist in that still point that
confounds life and death the center
of nothing brilliant swirling ecstasies
of light constantly coming into being
as if no future were possible no child
no swarm of bees no depthless waters
whatever we are is but an afterthought
of the deity whose task it is to smoke
seated atop the pyramid of the Sun
counting the dust motes ablaze in
the labyrinth of air and before day
is done and the mountain has exhausted
its recollections of the Hour's end
that deity too has morphed into a
pattern of darkness eternal a sleep
that visits flittingly the Cyclops' eye
is everything a vast disorganized dream ?
not even the gods knitting their brows
in a hazy twilight of blissful unknowing
can figure out the why of entelechy
mushrooming flames of origination
voices that descend from a profound

confusion of elements tattooing the ether
with a syntax of enigma and thunder
why do we struggle to hold in our
hands these multiple effusions of light ?
on our knees we await the winged
ones the messengers of speech and
aphasia turning over in the ear
a syllabic disaccord of the heavens
is this the afternoon of great awakening ?
a summer passes in a dragonfly's shadow
bouquets of narcissus and hyacinth
steeples of marigold and sunflower
long meadows dedicated to Apollo and
the endlessly imagined sun on High !
it is too soon autumn and withering
leaf and branch bereft and ivy bruised
trailing in the purplish dusk of hills
far to the west of memory nowhere
really the vacuum of the gods
those pluperfect entities stunned
in the season that supersedes
                              time ,
and they who come after and wild
score the rocks and shoreline the buzz
hives and heath the porphyry brush
a headline declares anathema and war
anger of short-term memory witless
beings armed with spite and ire fists
on the opposite shore two shadows
watch infirmity and gauze of moonlight
the waters rising from sleep the haze
cannot determine which is and which
is not , the ones with names soon

forgotten and climbing out of earth
and in fields of obscurity and sounds
indeterminate to the ear the winds
and vacated statuary and the eye
solitary fixed on the revolving sphere
an idea a section of the untold memory
of things wondering the always of
the gods the possibilities of existing
without pronouns the sheer mystery
that one can come and go just like
that in a trice a wink a flash of light
between the boulders of eternity
, so come down from the on-high
the gods frivolous and embattled
preterit nations of phonology and
abracadabra putting a finger to the
wheel turning ever slower smoking
beneath the lids pictogram cinema
flickering vision embroidery phosphor-
escence of planets and zodiac plunging
into magma seas lava colloidal waves
to be born ! a length of time ago a
short breviary speaking sidewise a
dialect of Neolithic refrains a,
silencio !
at a simple remove from space
                    the gods !

iv

I reworded the adjectives replaced
the semaphores erased the punctuation
revised the syntax reread the page rewired
the nouns rewrote the vowels retracted
the consonants restricted the meaning
I rescinded virtually every letter of the alphabet
restructured the wedges rendered useless
the pictogram refueled the spaces in between
reorganized the beginning rephrased the
termination restarted the accents rebooted
the ontology in addition I rewound light
removed the zodiac realigned the calendar
reworked my brother realized dying and
then when dawn's utter flare reversed
I woke and began the machine put on the
engine stoked the fire redressed the orient
undressed the goddess reemployed the oracle
opened my left eye first looked for the gamma
hooked my vision on the suture darkness I
plunged with my right eye stuttering with
both hands shifting the color red to its
total possibilities called the morgue talked
with the corpse in hieratic syllables but
understand nothing and hung up and walked
across the lawn and refigured the moon
waning in its diphthong I rephased the arc
settling for a hasp and a buckle and a small
nothing miscomprehending the whole
anchored the face in the mirror shaved the
shadow of its identity loosened the bolts

aimed the quiver prayed to Diana and
waited patiently on a blade of grass and
in one ear heard the surf denying and in
the other a simulacrum of Venus arose
shaking the dew from her hair and me she
took one look and fled into the ether I
paralyzed with love for the One knowing
nothing of the Other and absorbed in rapt
attention to the Sound spent the lifetime of
a day trying to and not succeeding and
startled by a leaf falling and resident stone
and profligate rock the eponymous epic verses
strung out in helium and in no way could read
the orphic reaction and winds and gales and
other tempests in the form of dead angels
both proceeding from and returning to clouds
sonant glyphs enormous cliffs abracadabra
aphasia and numinous directions gone wrong
a traffic of decibels and clangor and bongs !
to be at the very middle and have no sense of it
awash in puerperal fantasies of life on earth
coming to be and holding in awe the trees
the leafage the ivy crawling rampant around
the goddess' waist and singing in rapture the
madness apogee of a dialect in fever and reading
rereading rewording retexting rewiring *what ?*
the ethereal inscription that occurs only once
before dissolving in recriminations and water
I repented reliving that portion of the page
with no exit but exulting oblivious to and
remindful of the running aground of language
inextricable phraseologies of floral contests
long drawn out hours of recitations in archaic

to an audience of statues maimed for their
abilities to speak and hear and wonder !
this too will pass
this too will pass

V

you ask how much more can I have to say
I answer when is there an end to grief and sorrow
is there an extension to the peninsula of gas ?
does the play-book include burial rites and ash ?
when the fixtures came undone and the overhead
bulbs flickered cluing us to the subterranean moment
and all around asphodel and shadow and the great
marmoreal effigies of oracular but unknown divinities
the whispering and worship of the god of hips and irises
the fluid journey that takes memory out of its skin
remembrances of flute and bone and hair in the wind
wounds caused by infrared and eschatology of water
when will there be nothing left to comment
to remark to footnote to amend to obliterate
because sleep does not fit the afterlife nor gloves
keep off the stuttering from hands too mysterious
to recount and the secret infernal blazing implicit
in the unwritten poem about the unexpected disappearance
the vacuum remaining in the room emptied of life
light and breath oxygen and nitrous and acids that score
and the bilious events one never wants to recall
the accident on the sidewalk the overturned wagon
the white oxen felled by Apollo on the hillside
meadow and bas-relief of mortuaries afternoons
too fogged and bays in search of a shoreline you ask
if there isn't a way to cease thinking to absent
the self from life's squandered years the isoglosses
and maps of dialect retreat and taking the body back
if possible from the pool of regrets the absolute pitch
in the tone of a song about to be recorded in a studio

far from the regulations of silence the crooning
and mourning who will establish the definitions
increase the frontiers put an end to sand and the ants
who are the carriers of dark colors and distance
when will the entrance to paradise be anything but
the gasoline pump considered out of use and mileage
and décor and imperfection of the idea itself haunting
the remains of a mountain and pyramids and a stairway
who will be smoking the last cigarette talking
against a tempest of fireflies signing the air with warrants
to enter and slash and destroy the histories
those haphazard chronicles in vellum and or parchment
drizzling letters attempts at hagiographies in hieratic
nomadic script and the blazing furnace of intention
of rescinding the paragraph of remonstrance and
then when that is done and the beauties of verse
recited to the dream couriers who have breathlessly
descended from the seventh heaven on mounts
of a sandy hue in a lather and annotations about
Hercules and the spotted beast and the lair of myth
the violence inherent in the missing vowels the pidgin
speech of those who are busied with interring
the recent and unnamed war dead and the rivalry
of language and the unspoken word and viruses
that take the brain away from its lamp *how !*
you ask I cannot be the motion beside the stele
erected on the retroflex consonant of the southland
where we are bidden by the dead dearest to us
the inflexible gravity of the archaic atmospheres
that accompany us on the voyage downwards
to the excavations of the tenth city of Pluto
handing back and forth the corrupt readings of a text
a grimoire a flight-manual attributed to Hermes

you ask I cannot answer the endless refrain in the head
to wake and see the world is still too much with us
the plundered earth the multiply bruised planet
and the moon too circling its ineffable syllable
who can translate that who can keep in rotation
the dove-tailed mantras the dusky remote oriental
phraseology forever locked in the circular heat
that punctuates the summers of our farthest infancies
ask me I cannot you wonder what I have to say
writing this long the last of the lost epics

vi
was it the paragraph about insanity
that led you to different conclusions
to resignation and heartbreak the twofold
and the diameters of Helen and her moon
was it rumors and hearsay and dialect
of still another language employed
to describe the great mortal arc among
the embers of the already numberless
ghost planets refugees of a castoff red
warriors who have forgotten how they
got to the other shore the bedridden
and lousy paradigms of human frames
those shorn of memory and intellect
only the muffled sobbing in the walls
the ransacked mattresses of bedlam
the wound and the cauterizing agent
nurses striking for minimum wage
everything on backwards and nightfall
just past the noon hour and the failed
substances and x-rays and petroleum
windows that go round and round trying
to contain the sun and the pathetic echo
wheels running over gravel in anxiety
will the patient make it to midnight
will the text be finished and the eulogy
and the statue just dug out of the pit
will it begin to speak again in the famous
glyphs of Linear B and for sure Menelaus
and his brother and the forged decretals
of the fuming and angry deities pissed

that the apple was not awarded to them
and Hesperia and the shining mountains
and the Spain of Abd-er-Rahman dusky
with its patios and splashing fountains
where to go what to infer how to do it
insanity of life on earth geomancy and
intrepid columns of waste water and fuses
plugged into discharging units and
the iron lung and the horse meant to
carry the sky over the next ridge into
the fossil ditch and the intensities of mouth
lip to lip surgery aphasia and silences
of stone the very frontier of mind in its
cold aberration to define the soul vagrant
wand of winds blowing hither and thither
boreal and austral with names of those
interred in myth for want of a better end
yet bitter and the acrimony of promises
to continue and stepping gingerly
over the flower beds and glycerin and
protean transformations of dream into
following days and exhaustion of bone
and tissue dismemberment the body
who will want it back after so much ?
hush low the little whisper the edges
to vowels emitted in expiration
insanity that makes you conclude
this paragraph longing for the other
time the illusory inch of grassy slope
recollection and isotope of temporality
the world ! its shadowy denizens and
grief beneath the dozen passing suns
and sleep

vii

and here will be a great many of them gone
out of memory and of the comb and wattle
the steam-press and flat-iron the corporation
of deceit and investment human hunger lobes
and ear-strings the throat a dry channel
and bone-meal the fusion of darkness to night
who will never be recalled nor for want
of money and the slight anger of the peninsula
and the boats drawn up like insect husks and
odor of pitch the vermin spawned by purulence
on the skin who will entreat the blind seers
with their prayer wheels and old voices now
gone from the chords and the drifting tune
gone into the leaves and from afar hear
the drawn decibels of brass and mercury
once loud now the taint of ancient sulfur fumes
the incomplete hole where was the entrance
to the House of Pluto the wailing and of the
many more gone nameless the placard of Fame
besmirched with lies and treachery this was
earth and its continents sewers and infamy
gutted porches and the dirk and task of assassins
a sounding in the eerie hour of the ambulance
towering vestiges of theater and spoon a rock
standing in the form of a question where a tree
should have grown with its spreading summer
how can there be a re-entry to the sky numinous
and vanishing like smoke into the vast empyrean
stars by day torching the fanes of gods too decrepit
to care enunciating and spokes of the Circle sprung

from the axle the brooding and manipulated treasurer
the divan of discord and the Muse errant bereft
of her once dazzling raiment thumb to thought
chin poised to airs of violence and the mistaken
identities the alphas of aboriginal discontent
why are the seasons come to an end in their music
viol and rebec and sistra the taproot and drum
tom-tom voodoo of dusk when plangent orchids
appeal to the first stars of the west to come !
dance and fade of those lying in wait by urns
and counting ashes syllable by syllable and high
their arms suppliant to the Venus of the apogee
shedding light over the false countries of Mu
legend and ossuary where the blind pick through
discarded hieroglyphs in the hope of salvation
can a mere sound the repetition of a vowel
in obfuscation gives us redemption ? ask and
ask again the ones in the vestibule of Harmony
nowhere but the yellowing and sere foliage
the ivy gone to rot on the stucco and the cry
of the peahen mourning its sequestered mate
brings on the rain-cloud the torment at sea
the blustering icon of byzantine error and manufacture
what once was and now the quaint relic of
a country church a fuse attached to the root
where stone gropes for light the all-encompassing
is there to be another day a fortune of whistles
a mystery quaking at the seams some shape
of ink that will absorb the loss of memory ?

11-11-18

viii

tormented winds that take breath away
blow today as on no other smoke-consumed skies
weather vanes ripped from the socket roofs
and trees tributaries of rock and stream
whole meadows of pasture grass and flowers
in their contest for beauty torn petal by petal
like vowels snatched from a litany of verse
sacred and profane how many too many to
count the now dead bereaved behind glass
entombed reduced to inhabit urns other spheres
zones where mingle hair and strange music of
and the Pan on the rocks and the scourge
why is so much gone in a whisk ? was here
the metal solid and over there a foundation
platinum scores celestial whistles diving
matter the section of water divorced from
liquid and the haze all amazing potential
dying in the constancy of light a leaf at a time
immemorial sounds legends rushing through
ears of stone and Calliope dressed as a parasol
swept away by a corner of invisible traffic
hands down the end has come and gone and
who saw it happen who was transfixed and singing
almagest and tribunal and zodiac revolving
on the fingertip of the mountain and sorrow
the back yards and screen doors slamming
shut and keys lost in snow the motor that
won't start and whoever else fell from memory
weathers that go back to last week then
vanish into a space lit by neon planets flares

beacons flashing red on and off the lonesome
and mysterious ride back from a nightspell
legends of clothing embodiments of persons
becoming and talking imitating statues
gods who flicker in windows gaming and loss
who govern the poultice and the indigo
for why does this happen now ? what is it ?
which of the many deaths Arianna has suffered
is the correct one and the Minotaur and
the hero Theseus and the island of Naxos
a story repeated in its syllables & digression
I wish I were an angel from on high !
take this baedekker and show me the way
blue pivots into red sensational news half
a legion away from the other half in a house
cold with dismay and shuttered for grief
does the elbow suffer more than the hip ?
ministrations of gasoline and asphodel the land
missing from the text about Nostalgia the fade
and athirst sailing from the center and mad
who partook of the cattle of the sun and warned
and now nailed by heat to slivers of matter
going round in the whirlpool with only a mirror
and waiting for evening and the first stars
the north of imagination entelechy and rude
lunations abuzz with hive and ant-heap
recollections of a terra firma immersed
in oils a distance of words unspoken of scansion
and meter and circumflex and isolation
will we ever get back to the starting point ?
it is remote and animus and echo alike
going to sleep like that so alone forgotten
could not have him back the interloper

who went in and out of our lives like a thread
sewn into the skin of passion and paled
a minute ago and was gone the next

11-11-18

ix

what to steer clear from every angle
the rising dark like unbidden waters a
shape emerging a dim specter with stop-watch
and lip balm and the towering edifice
where they go to seal the urns and caskets
we set sail by midday on the last trireme
bound for Crete such as illusions are
the radio and the Fax machine the oiled
gears the gods use to fool mortals into thinking
and the predigested syllabary vacuous afloat
in the meridian haze the sirens of distance
and the mountain rearing its feathery mind
saying this is the way and this is the end
this is the sky and these are the other skies
I touch and float with my rootless thoughts
inventing a time that never was a child
a tree a stone an abyss into which all fall
thus the mountain in its mantic state and
off unfurled the sails and oars dipped into
the briny and listened loud to the curses
vowels unchained and other unintelligible
sounds echo and resonance and sleep-talking
mementos of the oracle who wide-eyed in
trance spoke backwards to the mirror of
our travails a foil to the counterweight
girl chorus sings *sail away sail away sail away*
long swoon of sea thrumming in detached ear
feet long left the surface of gravity in flight
tender swills billowing whitening angry surf
did not remember to cut the ropes ? AOI

so on and so on the dismembered body
of the dolphin crimson streaks in the wake
who is responsible for incurring the god's wrath ?
were I to wear this mask until the morrow
would my pronoun no longer fit ? I steal
the husk from its shadow and hail high
portents and disguises and matchless robes
a-swirl in infinite gaze of the Foam-born one
the et cetera of countless days the epitome
of a wasted life the lyres and beckons and sweets
whose blanched arm wrapped around me
a dream of freshet and eye-pools deeper than
anything where drowning was like entering
light and love's festoons and skull-garlands
nervous waking to a monotonous drum roll
sheets cast aside livid spots covering pale
skin and a song an eerie remonstrance
radio attuned to reports from the East
temple sanctions lifted boys dragged by heels
around the corporate walls of the tenth Troy
everything in disorder archaic dialect tones
sing-song pidgin idiolect monsoon warnings
and crepuscular fadings all across the border
having passed the tropics and now coming into
ports of the dead draped with ant-colored clouds
somber and funereal gestures of ancient kings
prepared to toss their frames into seething pitch
how came we to this destination ? southland
mournful trumpets behind the shaved hills
lonesome winding down of things elemental
colors pale into a lunar absence of evenings
beneath a heaven tortured by its own vanishing
starstuff doomed legendary planets unnamed

plummeting into the vast and what of the arc
the symbol and the grace to survive ?
unconscious tools of the sacred half-words
unspoken thongs stretched of the void an ellipse
empyrean of the beyond of time flickering
messages that tattoo the winds barking upheaval
when they come to take our bodies out of
the carcass of dawn ruin of fire and ether
come to sniff at us the infernal dogs a remark
seems to ricochet in the mind's brief alpha
a painful whatever it was drained from air
chorus of girls *sail away sail away sail away*

11-12-18

                    X
the kings the dynamo of dying the prefix
and the suffix and what comes in between
the small light the wisdom bole the accent
marred by sleep falling from one parapet
to the next lower one the symbols inferred
a hand holding the only other hand possible
of dying the subtext the array of half-words
curtailed syllables vowels abbreviated for
their intrinsic nonsense separated from
and in isolation of the word intended to imply
sections of air currents of breath running
between the what did you expect of night ?
tamer of horses ! guide the fates to their
own ashes mark the end of the vestibule
of space with a nacre exclamation point !
devour the tail of the self in a constant
renewal rising from the old skin lying there
in the slough and beware the traffic of red
lights stopping unexpectedly and loud the
memory of the sheer five thousand foot cliff
with its history of lithograms and fossils
reminiscence of the sea that created them
do you recall that long summer and the ferns
and the subtle remonstrance of rock and
water sliding over the parallel of time
the faint echo from the future of warriors
gazing into the mirror of their shields
a prism and pre-history of engines set into
the dark and to capture the mind in its offset
the press of creation sounding immense a

fiery bric-a-brac of fluids and ethers a huge
you might say weren't the horses too much
ablaze rushing through the nostrils of their
creator *Nemesis* the broken star of futility
to get back to the origins to pattern death
after its own sequences of acceptance and denial
come rest here beneath this spreading alder
let the autumn sun fan its wan rays over
the remains of the word *yes* all eyes on the road
the warning that deer might appear at the least
steering your vehicle swerving from rust into
the metropolis of trees great and ominous in
the morning of accidence which to choose from
among the many classics the illustrations of
the fallen just outside the ringed wall of Troy
beaches and southern discomfort of the poets
making the best of the few consonants left
at their disposal in the *aula magna* you will
be sure to write down the few utterances dreamt
in the chasm and when you saw the multiply
damned like barrels of fish belly up in brine
the limbo of those who never had a chance
those who never asked for a birthright and
were never given a chance to fend for themselves
between the two mountains and the aurora
the significant lamp of the orient God wasn't
that an error the myth and mismanagement of
clouds in puerperal fever the radiant glow
of inconstancy behind the marmoreal *appearance*
you could be a statue too or a machine monster
on the stage of deliverance and walking among
illusive the many personae to go to bed then
unaware the last time is upon us the upheaval

and journalism of Armageddon jump up
start the motor we have hours to go before
understanding nothing of the why and the stars

11-15-18

xi

we are no younger than the day we died nor
do we quicken up the cordillera's spine
to witness the dawn's gorgeous apparel
instead gathering fog and clouds and incense
burned over three days old we clamber
aboard some Chinese junk to embark on
the perilous voyage across the straits of *limbo*
pushing towards the cavities and peninsulas
of the unknown continent of unreckoned verse
tomtom and silhouette ink and hemlock
ivy that twines around the lost finger of time
a vast echoing in the small revolving ear
set in stone where we are bidden to reunite
sand and grass and leaf the mighty forces
we once knew with names like Diomedes or Ajax
and flung a spear and caught with her knee
exposed Artemis of the silver shafts did we but
know this was the first of the many deaths
swirling unresolved in the foeman's eye
whizzing through lambent air beautiful the dart
to claim us each unawares in the tossed meadow
of desire and longing lay the head down did
we on crescents of rock and sighing multiplied
the phantom sleeps we still struggle to remember
foil and stratagem of dreamers page and index
mementos of light and enormous steps carved
out of mind's unreformed thought the idyll!
do we sit cross-legged transposing heads ?
is there a moment when we do not defer to glass ?
what is it we inhale though incapable of breath ?
across the bow she shifts her fearful arm

in remission we will never be hunted down
white transmissions of the undefined soul
enigma and pitfall legends written invisibly
upon a skin of vanishing air former shapes
lingering like clouds in the sky's small remnant
do we flit like flying ants in dusky penumbra
mastering the skill of hills and earth behind
which is the prefered among the twenty evenings ?
where is the solace of the basalt pool where
come small dappled deer to reflect and drink ?
are we those animals painted on a fleeting day
numbered and uncounted the possibilities
like stars sighted on the restless wave and drowned
no sooner named than forgotten in an ecstasy
to remember what cannot ever be again shining
and residence of immortal spirits moving in
and out of marble blocks vague intimations
desirous of becoming statues caryatids acanthus
embroidering a history of unwritten thought
come ! so many the capsized in a thimble
so many more the elusive who dwell inside
the color red the bright and variable shifts
tone and sequence of unbidden sounds echoing
between the rills of abandoned waters a whole
prehistory of litmus and disappearing the youth
of us the unformed who proceed from absence
enormous yet indistinct in inchoate dust
shape of what lies outside of space boundless
nostalgia for the missing summer the unfound
lake the sawdust and midges of eternity
feeding on the edges of a grassy tract extended
far into the unconstructed sarcophagus of light

11-15-18

xii

not nymphs nor the gladiolus "sword"
the unencumbered how do we get over the water
to have remembered even a quarter of what
was taught in the art academy and fling
our oils and pitches on the canvas drilling for
air even if it were possible to define what it is
respiring in the coal mine of life where small
maps indicate only an ant could manage
a mountain in fact both mountains rearing
their feathery sombreros a message to Orestes
a hummingbird in the relief of an eye colored
so brightly not even the sun its noon blaze
here where summers are measured by the minute
a hand a crawling sphere a fandango associated
with serpentine and the queen of hell Herself
the portent the stone upon which sits the gilded
tomb the hierophant and his double the executioner
with his hacksaw and belt and the courier bearing
diplomas to the pilgrim in the hill why do we
test these envelopes wear this hair share this
and that as well the heaving voluptuary dawn
interrupts with such hues ranging from lavender
to ocher and the god who sits in the middle
all thumbs the cadaver tied to his wrist alone
talking to the rooster and the fantastic chair
propped up midterm where sun meets his
mortician the doll in Sufi rags appointment
with the oracle mirror and spit and frenzy
wild appellation of the tarot dealer tabled
to spin the tale in retroflex consonants and aphasia

double shift of the syllable that stands for moon
the great circumflex of ink the aspiration to be
other in the next life the wearisome wasn't that
enough to drag the body through such torments
fever and x-ray and the various dope to control
epilepsy a hero couldn't have lasted as long
as his own shadow in the defiles where Mars
and his phantom persona whirl quoits and hiss
it was frail and priceless it was life but could
we save it ? numb and deaf lean and lost
our child gone into the morning mists a wheel
out of reach an altar and the yoked ox brought
to the knife and letterhead a splash its blood !
siphon what you can of the light and sift it
spleen and vertigo dust in histories of west
the last and lost forces on the beast's brow
inscriptions as inscrutable as they are red
lasting totems the token wars in its eyes belittled
ciphers pleading for a release from shape
all that ever was of the lithograph of space *hark !*
lightning rod held fist-tight in the deity's
empty hand and as ever I close this epistle with
the darned socks of evolution the quire and ream
the blank efforts of the page to find punctuation
assays and forgeries of the planets out of orbit
evidence that chaos is its own format precipice
and proemium fugue and thistle crown of ether
'til death do dumb part as quoted by the seer
in the burning bush and then daylight its loss
fundamentally a will o' the wisp or firefly
the soul the human yearning to transcend
matter the depth and the dark and the back
to the start the ships in medias res the shoreline

the cast of thousands in diminished type font
ampersand and clepsydra crescent ivy whirls
please the next line the diameter and push
Muse O ! legend has its decline and fever and
so little else to tell the river about its toll
small fingers rushes a privy sense of endings
which to choose and whispered onyx detail
what blind bard his sequel and dying breath

11-15-18

xiii

what were you doing at the crossroads last night
was it wearing for the lost minute Hecate's symbol
blood red moon and total sadness to bear a lifetime
the revolver still hot but unconscious in the left hand
was it memory of a war time without your participation
the offal and incandescence ignited by greed or lust
underwent some kind of surgery kept an eye open
though if only to identify the leaf among the moons
a greenery of spent relic ivy formidable wrapping
a scimitar of light tightened around someone's throat to
confess *I didn't wanna do it* opalescent dots streaming
through the night-wear ants and midges craving
a finger of flesh you struggled to discern differences
but only encountered the difficulties being alive and
breathing between monitors still clicking on and off
in a room of total anonymity shadows busying themselves
with water rock and sand the precipice like albumen
whitening what remained of the oriental horizon
broken windows taped motors to the skin a chart
representing the rise and fall of fever and a doctor
impersonated by a radio voice using a Latin system
of pronunciation and the howling of maddened
mothers in their balconies wondering O why did I
let him go my winsome Johnny and in reverse flags
flapping stars asterisks penumbra they say of gods
who fatigued by mortal dissensions want back wings
to fly from the human galaxy to some port of entry
to inferno itself a pleasure palace an inscription with
aspirin and the convexities of reason still on display
tatters of rags and seers in buskins and porphyry

staggering on a make-shift stage speechifying loud
into the pre-natal slumber and what could you make
of it the boulder on either side the stairs only half-
way the cigarette burning in the saucer and lipstick
in cuneiform all over the nurses darkened face shades
of lavender and puce *please* cries someone from Beyond
you ruffle through curtains beside the bed wondering
the other world the subtext of gratitude and fear a *life*
perceived from the outside the thin vowels connecting
the realm of the dead that great southland with the
next version of the story and the characters in grief
lining up to see for the last time the victim in his
small bed of rushes and reeds murmur of underground
stream and lamenting of nymphs everything a dusky
aversion a template of ampersands meant to burn
come the dawn and the foals and whinnying of invisible
beasts and portents the Nightmare at the crossroads
whom you embraced uncertain of the doctrine of light
how many times could it matter or even happen months
apart from the mountain and the summer residency
when you stepped in onyx pools regarding from afar
the hieroglyphs the painted jaguars the leaping fawns
through an atmosphere of archaic ash still falling after
the recent eruption and the new islands and the stillness
unabated mysteries the potential lamp and its abstractions
who would write to you from that distance in letters
carved from sandstone and ivory a reticence as the doors
shut and a hand from the clouds extinguished the flare
that had persisted in the doorway // a way out a sequence
of footfalls a sussuration to the ground where an ear
sculpted out of a pink shell the great silence of the sea
which you are bound to enter come day's end

xiv

and kept coming in saddle-stitched memory
echelons , the tender who came forward and
elicited first rounds of fire the beach and
anchored craft at their back , famous for
its smoky walls the town and its citadel
ahead of them already a dim silhouette in
the man-created haze a roaring , shifting
of proportions of red to azure and the clouds ,
what was their name Antenor or Patroclus
a once hero in greaves brass shiny , dust in
choking squadrons fling of spurs and spears
horses alighting from mounds the hills hiding
what others there were in parchment , to be
read in lists by even-tide the hearth a nostalgia
for books long forgotten spines sutured in
flakes of alder bark or salt chips and dots
resemblance to the stars , furious ampersand
of the night heavens the Pleiades and the Bear
huge remonstrances , like dreams , repetition
and inversion simultaneity and chiaroscuro
as the legend goes , dream within a dream
chasing the dream of *being* , and when thought
none more were to come assembled in midst
of wave and glyph the mighty with oar and
shield buckled to mortal arms the brazen
whorl in the sky blazing like a cyclopean
eye , immeasurable destiny and fatal purling
against the noon cycles of heat and enormous
their cry , the spectacular beams and targets
the imitation of beast muzzled frothing , odium

and pleasure alike emerging from the opening
pages of the book , scores of them in full armor
clad and as if asleep yet marching in disarray
, elements of ether in equal halves and soon
frozen in their fates to become quarry to a
goddess the argent one in blowing skirt a thigh
revealed to the dying , to see with their lips
what stone was rent from earth tongue torn
from root vowels scattered in the lymphatic air
as if bleeding , skin and grass and hair mouths
full of earthen breath to smother whose wives
left behind forewarned to mourn , knee and hip
consigned to the bards' eloquent consonant and
ribs shattered in a poetry of broken equilibrium
a matter darkened within the hour and distance ,
alone and with sorrowing in the leaves and as
mind gathers its remains and wonders to forget
a city a republic and acropolis altars fuming and
lard greasing the atmosphere the stench of praise
to the gods whose witless demands have caused ,
like as not sleep will not be easy and why aren't
the captives in line like disordered punctuation
and what seems modern the ravages of intellect
blank verse and bad pronunciation , here's delta
and beside it the river mouth foaming and an order
impossible to understand the bright and pink
the overwhelming absences and not a friend in
sight not a , campfires put out water at a reference
point to be distilled outcrops of madness illusory
women with small bound feet and speaking an
oracular form of Chinese in the twenty first
century already where we pivot in our snapped
sandals and brick in hand hurl against the Unseen,

chronicles in loose microform detailing ascent
of kite and dirigible and the invention of guns
and the entire panoply of assassination and revolt
the swift descent headfirst and oblong and
ultimately terrifying Avernus ! shock white the
pallor of their faces muzzles unshaven chins jaws
splintered in the ovation all hail to the king the
bravado and size of his ink and the sadness , really
all that's left of the day in tiny glass vials , image
and highway of the phenomena called man the
absorbed in the self the smaller and lesser , who
will recount this the day with its triptychs and
syllables painted only to fade a pale the western
etched the dross echoing stellar drones a thing
worn bone thin and sprawled over rocks life-
less of memory and fell swoon to Hades

XV

hunger and loss—the world grammatical
deviation the shock of the reversal pinpoint
reflexes nerve endings and fiction of the polity
can as such the bulbs go out and the trip more
than once to the medical joint the bone shop
the meretricious waiting at the door with their
wolverine eyes and gaudy painted mouths
lipping vowels and obscenities tongue on
the cornice the valve turned way up can't hear
so well the prescriptions for oral devices
for concatenations of cold sores of unconsciousness
could not salvage from the burning wreck even
a pair of souls the long unwinding fluted columns
excess of consonants writing a prognosis in red
ink the constabulary of reason overturned midnight
the incessant rains sulfurous and atmospheres
turned to pitch black the sovereign lamp slowly
its back turned and the prestidigitators at the corner
want to sell a copy of Marx and cheap vaudeville
stunts hand in mouth disease the poor guy lying
there on his bed of nails waiting to be jabbed
one more time like in the history books the march
up country Xenophon and the later dialogues
gnosis and revelation the lessons issuing from Persia
idiomatic translations of the Zend Avesta *hunh ?*
later on when the hour seems to wear thin they
put on their surgical gloves and mask their putty
smiles fist full of some kind of denigration they
who watch civilization and its discontent wryly
remarking on the fodder and the illusory oil

deposits and the off-shore drilling while up
in the ICU they keep asking the comatose guy
if he knows where he is what time it is what's his name
and so forth the windows shed a semantic glare
soon it's time for the windup the loudness of
at least five machines gonging and binging all
together and at once the chaos of modernity which
Machiavelli invented the comedy of errors in a root
to be digested come supper time and wash their
skins and order tickets for the opera *sang froid*
so much and so many they can't keep up the count
how many deaths the red-skin the buffalo the water waste
when the Oregon trail was young and they found
frozen the amazing fossils of truth and dignity
scalped and later sold to Barnum and the Ringlings
a shape of air scalloped out with their gizmos
medical paraphernalia the Greek aorist included
studying to become skilled barbers excising
from the human remnant a part that will go to the moon
superannuated and minuscule the ethical portion
tomorrow a deviant hour announced will possibly
bring down the earth as we know it the massive tumor
building up in the soft-drink industry and finally
who's to say that the person on the operating table
isn't your brother after all ?

xvi

the ellipse haunted the few of the last
remaining to see their wan figures the pale
it was living there on the promontory
the fading and wasted listening for the
late whistling through the branches night-
birds the hooting and asked to return
on footpaths softening the lisping leaf
above the head how could we endure
that life those minutes unending the sad
even moon at its height and reddening
sorrow's brief letter written and rewritten
on the backside in shorthand the flux
of events the acrimony and anxiety the
more than ever pallid something underbrush
a ring of light evanescent the sky itself
how could we stand it at either end the haze
the burnished tapers the blundering knee
a wavering wasn't it inconstant and
at the summit of the hill a clump of trees
denuded solitary a signature we said of the
whatever we left behind why did we keep
moving foot after foot the loss still too heavy
to bear how much the human soul and
trying to recall where it all happened why
the lever didn't work where the valve was
and the leak and the pool overflowing a
dense subterfuge they say it was a history
for the books a sequence highlighted by
news from the other side of skiffs deployed
to carry them to the unseen and unknown

vowels of eerie resonance the small Latin
expressing grief and what of the poets whose
names lost in syllables errant woods the broken
oracle bone-smooth nothing apparent even
to the touch of fingertips and wasn't there
a meadow once and the way a voice born
on the slope a darkening waste a mere
or a phrase recondite and somnolent
both the trussed bedding the wisps of hair
the brow matted feverishly damp the wail
the impossibility of recognizing who that was
yet grieve we did the sequence of knot and
knuckle the tale and its fractured trail
of words denominations verbal prefixes
and especially the wounds implicit in the
scansion the vertebrae of echoes missing
a beat here and there we looked and listened
floundering in denial and absence the which
and the what and the why they kept teaching
rote and round of sound and symbol a loud
a vaster than it is wide broader than it is
tall the figurines the lapsed statuary of ether
and gas the evidence that perhaps no one
had been here before us the first to enter
leaving behind the rusted gates barely hinged
why was it winter in our isolation a solace
that the sun still rose the portent of things
in flight wings shifting slowly in hue and tone
a phase reluctant to wear ghostly the raiment
to summon a goddess from her smoke and
read the entrails and evening suddenly before
the vacancies of water a tolling of the dead
in their enormous bell and the cuprous fringes

a byzantine estuary up to the waist
and still moving slogging a marsh a delta
a mourning in each glyph as sleep with its
ineffable mythology of ink descended and
oblivion one by one the stars extinguished
how could one hear what could one know
eclipse and childhood of the cosmic endings
a great mystery laying the head down
rock and reef and wild cliff of memory

xvii

fury of strings the concerto and hydraulics
spilling over into the dream and for an instant
a reckoning the far distances of sleep Dionysos
composed of wild oriental clouds astride a leopard
to visit the hospitals and stews of the western orb
hemispheres of air and the oblique parting of
the skies into unequal darknesses the shifting
of allegiances among the gods petty in their
bawling and roaring the tragedy coming to be
defined as a goat dance a bloodied pelt to be
worn by the king nominated for a day and
small fires in their eyes the satyrs watching
with dismay the figure suddenly fallen to stone
despite the foaming mouth the once lithe limbs
now crippled forever in the death grip a fell
swoon the leaves about to bleed torn from branch
isolated penumbras lesser waters in the backdrop
a fear of gas and sand echoes of a wind soughing
between the ears and whatever else the destined
word can reach between one mountain and the
other rearing their fossil domains high into night
how came this story and what of the ash and lever
the hidden lake the route and the schedule winding
between dry river beds and immense cavities
legends of unremembered wars once the epos
and fancy of dreams now deadened silences
painted weathers of farthest stars the reaches
of infancy strained by discord and abandonment
punctuations that separate the possible from
the infinite and all the sundered vowels become

blanks in the interrogation of the soul as it
prepares to embark on a passage of quicksilver
while masks shivering from a previous life peer
puzzled at the enigma of a future that variable
unending cycle of mysteries

                                        hesitation doubled
at the knee claustrophobia and x-ray of the mind
red in its multiple schemes afloat and
whatever else eludes grasp and Dionysos
bent over the pool watching the fish
that dart through the Cyclops eye
tiny fists of lightning
exploding

xviii
it was the night of fireflies and stars
of green alcohol hills of fading and dense
the lying back-wise stoned in the adolescence
of tridents and batteries dead to the swoon
of light to the slope and handcuff of waking
dream-spent slumber-doomed the dawn
of citrus integers hooves dust swirling
to thought no grievance and the alimony
of planets lost to the frame of time a lone
and wandering powder swirling skirts aflame
who could say it would end down under
brush fires and stone ridges on the verge
of collapse ant-eaten moth-warped swarms
of stunned bees in the shape of ink folded
into its own buckle the stain and sprawl
of life freed from its metal-band a hasp
rusted to the core and bone splintered
in echoes of the first thought ever of seas
the shore of a single finger outlining mind
the brick and wail suffering days to do
what language can no longer the confusion
particle and dot sequence of irrational
mythic and slender the balances in the skies
heavenly proportion to grief stellar reduct
between each muscle of plangent worries
why this had ever come defined as lawns
and the fast answer to lightning unhoped
for theaters demesnes of the unconscious
where sit side by side demon and child a
wine of intense images flickering on the

fade screen portents of an afternoon solid
of stone and cliff the wave a single lifted
by mechanisms of beauty into a painting
the perhaps of caryatid and siren louder
even as the ambulance creates its own speed
owning to streets of mortar and epistle
readings of a grimoire in the eccentricity
of the Hour flashes of a memory in leaves
written in back-hand by the goddess of mirrors
a spike of fire a flare of nasturtiums a water
doubled by its own reflection in the drowning
of *Echo* and the mountain itself interposed
between atom and black matter sophistic
tides rushing to maroon the spare traveler
on his raft eyes of wax and deaf to sunlight
how many caverns and noons ? the distances
the remotest epicycles of a shoulder in search
of its hemisphere will this retrograde be you ?
fictions and sphinxes riddled by a kilogram
metallurgy of the pain it takes to recall how
the meter was to be checked and then evening
inevitable concussion of moons whose names
visit the daily nymph and bare the knee to
a violence of combs and running up-hill
remember to forget the echelons of hair
given to the fanatic zephyrs of a lost summer
here where embroideries of perfume and onyx
develop one by one the inch of the terminus
it is being a man fusion of the ineluctable
with the ephemeral of newsprint desire
whatever the ungiven and protocol spreading
its preterit tense across green alcohol
the firmament of adolescence and death

xix

between archaic rock and stone the enigma
proceeding with Dionysos and his gaggle
of rioting girls loud the air of procession
jangle of sistra drum and tambourine a
ululation between notes strident flute
wafts of beauty sheer as bright new silk
red that maddens like a puerperal fever
cheeks lusty with bright and effusion of
eye-blackener pouring in the noon cycle
of steam itself dense the purplish ominous
of distance unobtainable and cloud-stuff
organdy and faded denim inside out high
with the mysterious chorus of the souls
of the dead winding and weaving through
porous rock and crystal like memories
of sand sifted slowly through lost fingers
unable any longer to count the minutes gone
vacancies of ghost-alphabets written in sky-azure
to be memorized by nightfall and the girls
grazing the epitome of their right to life
and statues busts of crazed emperors marble
fictions of the greatest of antiquities in oblivion
master of thurible and incense Dionysos
fluid and feminine touching each soft secret
in his passage to India his mind like the miles
of vast wavy blond hair in lava swept Sicily
a night once more in the vagabond waters
a trident and a fish-eye pierced by hidden suns
lure of death in gorgeous fluxes of black tide
who wouldn't want to enter in his train the

flowing and voluptuous architecture of wind
having sex with torments of ivy wild blown
colors crocus and porphyry and lavender
sewn into the hairpieces of the girl-swarms
a mystery of dream and initiation and dying
all at once in the single attitude of heat perched
on a mountain-top just outside the entrance
to space and the rush of invisible planets and
a zoo of stars and predictions at first ineffable
then in a quiet dissension of ether clear and white
like a drizzle of neon lasting for just a brief
second of eternity the whole and the nothing
abracadabra of combs and lip-gloss and wires
incandescent shifts of hills and jungle mesh
there is no destiny no fate of man no oracle
only the presumption of birth before death
maze of liquids and crevices hermeneutics
drilled like asterisms into a history of air all-
mothering that surrounds the mortal conjecture
moon-sheen blanks souls of the dead clapping
silently in day-shine somnolence of Dionysos
the great triumph and cosmic end-all
yellow dazzle fizz of booming surf
and darkness that floods the small ear
before sleep ignites the labyrinth of time

XX

where light intersects with light making
the past multiple dizzying reflections
in a sequence of broken mirrors the
present never coming to bear and future
already prey to fireflies and madness
a vision left better sleeping in the niches
where myth folds and unfolds its sheets
spreading them out on the lattice work
of the vineyards and what Ho old beast
comes roaring from his lair and mind
erupts on its peninsula puzzled that
so many persons can inhabit a single cell
skies revert to the closed door of antiquity
marble hewn from an abstract palimpsest
erected repeatedly in the heat of noon
and talking the always figurines of dust
unequivocal vowels left static in midair
and ether divided into north and south
the shuddering of the thunderbolt alive
and louder still refrains from the arena
counting the many emperors created in
a single day and the lust and shout and
bright of historical misrepresentation
nothing can be accounted for but illusion
the child in the furnace the tale of a horse
monarchic sperm left on the wharf to dry
absinthe lace and the mountain projected
in the hour to come and shadows flitting
escaped from the gasoline of death but
still uninformed as to the self and body

while you and I deluded in our museum
walk round and round the precious trunk
branch and leaf the names of hidden cities
trying discern the lives of heroes in glass
small letters glyphs and burnt porphyry
and embolisms of the gods swift course
through the nave fractures of archaic
the atmosphere and its hazy continents
periplus and itinerary of the Sirens
the ear ecstatic with the longing echo
arisen from the crevices of dulcet rock
dewfall and splinters stuck in fingers
and grass that lingers like a stain on air
evening with its fevered star marks silence
with a bell of crystal impermanence AOI
visionary phrases unuttered left in ink
that spills the margins from their heights
and we two still perplexed in the Sound
originating from all four cosmic quarters
move this shift and that sleep-talking dumb
perpetually caught between *now* and *then*
jewels of a text extracted for their sheen
imitation moons in name only and best
unread in long lines of pure hexameter
unfurled canvases parchments daubed in red
inches to the left behold ! where light inter-
sects with the light of yore and deaf to
the catastrophe outside that bursts its wall
a pigment on each fingertip a thought
dissolved in the brain's puny labyrinth
you become some *other* a chronic skin
to be worn in the absence of memory
and I ?

xxi

universal sadness , the , spreading its
ink across all that was formerly and all that
no longer exists I hear , that , a grieving
in the leaves a willow steeped in waters
that are not there and skies always redundant
and wherever a summer has spent its heat
and months that pass nameless in a quadrant
of despair , there , a memory evaporates
a syllogism of shoulders heaving and stains
left and right the vital signs recorded and
erased , when , the room of empty phantoms
graces three the ladies that cannot be seen
and evenings in a single glass of liquid
amber shaped and cloudy , how , a hand
that cannot reach and fingers cease to count
the myth in form and shape the outline
on the wall , where , a system of tears and
cheeks and hair kept in separate envelopes
slid under doors and footsteps , here , like
a rush of leaves and grass spoken in a wind
born in gravel and whose map extends
far into night when least expected , why ,
a legend written upside down in a vacant
type font and lessons recited before dawn
in dreams of puzzling stone , then , a part
of air comes undone and renders its western
hills and weeps into the sheets colored by
a brush of vowels that hesitate as if sound
would never echo more the vast , again ,
it keeps returning through crystal and hellebore

and rings of solid ether and moon that
pierces the elevated lake a grove where Nymphs
shed their skin and dissolve in fluid syllables
a music that cannot be heard except by the
dying in their poetry , which , ancient as
mountain or earthen shifts the trembling
foot the lyre in suspense and whatever else
the mind conjures in its falsetto tryst
perhaps the ocher of an oracle or the faint
and pallid gem of thought , this , an engine
attached to verses yet unwritten or to paragraphs
of running glass the morbid underneath
of fern and pond and finally the aftermath
of life the breath entwined in childhood's
ivy rampant in the mist of sorrow , not ,
deceived as light on a perfect day when azure
cloudless blooms like a floral spray and once
the eye conceives and stills the increased inch
a bloom a print pressed on the hand , whence ,
delays then yields forevermore to darkness
in leagues of unfolding silence ,
eternity ,

xxii

the roof of the world where harmonies gather
music swimming in the air the palms scored
for violin and solo how many the voices atop
this glebe of instrumental shores and trees !
stopwatch of water glistening just minutes
after the hour exploded in the hair one by one
nereids and dryads playing harps of mercury
wafting up from cedar groves the sweet scent
of matters less than solid and fictions wild ablaze
and pages rebooted to erase their print out loud
the hasting and recorded skiffs from distances
set sail buoy and keen reef a treachery who
will the next bell sound and summon from his
liquid pantomime Zeus all feathers and flight
swooning through the meridian a bull to be
a wrestling gadfly a tortoise in its own wake
pulled from cut stone a small flower anemone
so many mysteries the account books disappear
a string is plucked the note unheard an ear in ruins
sleep's archaic devastation in painted winds aloft
who can capture the twice sung void and stencil it
behind the cliff ? these are regions of ozone wide
and verticalities of an unthought dawn a section
of porous crystal a version of the almagest in Spain
violent tones descend in the fugue of litanies
each god now a statue in arrears a peplos drifting
in breezes by a trident summoned and drowned
the many and unnamed whose feet elaborated
the whispered path to mythical darknesses
that wrap in soundless emotion the restless vine

the world ! the economy of red and swirling ZZZ
seers in the deserted tower command a tongue
bifurcated in its paradigm of echoes lonely past
a mountain sheer white blank rock a tiny river
escaping through coils of dusty verse and grammar
each petal a transparent stain in the oblique light
alabaster of the ethereal column fade symbol of
sun spots running through their dusky pyramids
each one is Mexico on the alert each assassinated
in its vertigo of streets and twins of serpentine
what else can a park in its celestial verdant offer
planting lush grass and weeds and shifting concord
to its marriage place summer splash of green drizzle
reveries leaving earth adrift in a concerto of surf
a fix a fast a plunging daytime planet a puzzle
set in hematite and turned to shapes of sand
sudden death funeral pyres and winged threnodies
thrice holy sanctum a choir of dun western hills
a noon spent in the triangle of winds and brass
furious appeal of devil moons to Demeter
for a last but one ticket to the Underground
sixty Nymphs of amnesia all nine years old !
what is holy what is savage what is uncontested
no music however sublime but cacophony
underbrush of deceit and untruth the façades
aphasia of the multiple endings and not *one*
with clarity to move gliding serenely into
the inevitable Beyond the inevitable Beyond
 scattered like yellow pollen into the winds

xxiii

great dusky the vowels of medieval Spanish
moors half-moons and swooning silks a-splash
by fountains born of a noon's cyclical heat
in what midst do horses roan and sweating black
come rushing from the middle of a syllable
high spirits mountains that have no backside
water with wings and depths of onyx and beryl
with emerald eyes the phantom daughter of Fez
drags sheets across the lapsed son the last known
to have worn the famous trigeminal consonants
like a sacred pall a thread a link invisible
yet red that binds the skies by even-tide and swarms
of stars flash their thieving lamps bereft alike
of breath and shape drawing from an unkenned past
elegant ivories of a future tense a conditional
that can never be articulated the fuming dots
the asterisks and trembling lips that curtains
divide into uneven halves of inexpressible love
the totality of dust the sheer volume of air
blanks and aspersions and words hidden by
their own meanings like cliffs taken from seas
and placed beside the small apothegm of eternity
hills approach by afternoon's third hour
and olive groves and poplars silver in the glare
at least twenty suns mark the Saracen gold
with a script of arabesque and longing sigh
each crystal ornament which is a day undone
soul in reflex passion of purple winding algebras
trapped in a saddle of stone the muezzin's voice
pathetic chain of syllables crying in the black

hemisphere of what an ear can hear afternoons
when women of quivering smoke expose their flanks
dying in a tumult of hair and bone-phrased earrings
anklets fallen to the turf and knights crazed
with reading too much in the grimoire of time
castles ! bees ! fanatic intelligence of the thumb
sun-burnt in the constant vertigo of the hour when
unseen emperors dressed in vulgar Latin rags
toss their massive manes in puerile disdain
trampling on the crozier and the bloody palm
it is twilight in the forbidden Alhambra of ciphers
water-carriers mount the heavens on dead burros
clank of chain and rust inscriptions of torn nails
fingers that go switching through harsh arroyos
poetry of the moon archaic hendecasyllables
guitars of assassins! but the son the last known
laid out like a song of quicksilver and iodine
his vanishing pallor his fade of ancient children
his loudness a thing of the vagrant past echoes
dimmer than the *amarillo* scored in a lizard's eye
now cold now frozen like an unthought melody
no language tone or dialect his beauty can dissect
but mourning like the ring-necked dove or
hue that passes from pre-crystal dawn into dew
     Mi Hijo !

xxiv

studying the design on the kitchen floor
you realize then that life defines death
it's in the blood to do battle with bulls
to levy arms against monsters from the deep
that tragedy itself occurs at three in the morning
broken stanzas in Latin corrugated darkness
breath that eludes the symphony of reason
captured for an instant light as a form
of electricity and physics intangible
as are the moments summoned from a past
of irreducible dimensions floral pattern
and isotope and the long arguing with fate
wanting back what was never yours to claim
the child the map the lover the refrain
going back to the unrepeatable same line
incomprehensible with its inflexions and caesura
how can the mind be so arbitrary and multiple ?
where is the person who only yesterday
offered his money his wallet his identity
to the stranger knocking at the back door
asking for a handout that would last eternity
Hippolytus ! releaser of horses your pride
took you over the cliff broken in three parts
fields drained your blood and the somnolent green
of the infinite minute what else is there to report
standing there hand out to receive alms
as if a music might erupt in the dense pre-dawn
the surfeit of memory rushing like a small wind
across your brow stranger and phantom
how tiny the houses all in a row emerging
from night's cloister for just a brief hour
the lamp of reflections shedding a pale luster

over the photograph album yellowing
in its infirmity and desire to be corporeal
birth and dying revolving in even smaller units
icons and faded paintings depicting stages
in the life of the Buddha or all the previous
lives in this kingdom or that posing sometimes
as an animal and others as prince or mendicant
wrapping thought around the inconceivable
and at the window the naked branch
wet mourning its loss of leaves scrapes
plaintively against the senseless glass pane
do you address as well that denuded symbol
hoping to retrieve from its mute biology
compass of meaning a north a misdirected mountain
whose error will somehow illumine your path
meditative and diffuse through the maze
of the coming day with its projections
of untruth and irrelevant acts
what you may keep asking yourself
what does it mean these firestorms and cloud
brigades and polluted obscurities of air
which is the right door to open and who
is the correct stranger to give yourself away
becoming in that exchange both the *other*
and the corpse who looks back at you
through the unlit glass studying the design
on the kitchen floor archaic pattern of language
and silence the tomb of all realities
time suspended from its gravity
space constantly rushing away from space
finger to mouth ear cocked for the tick
that never repeats itself
life defines death

XXV

beauties and rigors the light of day
sifted through a few raindrops a gorgeous
dimension somewhere in between myth
and its counterpart death the famous
equivocations known as history written
or merely misremembered the accidents
and pitfalls of birth and coming to be and
the enigmas one by one which elude you
sleeping or half awake in a cinema of
error and deceit you do step gingerly
wanting to be a prize a shape of electricity
a conduit through which moon phases pass
ineluctable contests with planet and asterisk
forces of nature the size of ink and just
as destructive to those still walking recalling
exactly the day to the hour when ZAP
it all came home the truth and its dumb fundament
no longer the agile membrane but the corpse
the still-life handsomely laid out in colors
borrowed from eighteen kinds of flowers
and loud the single vowel of angels weeping
in plain chant and the harpist and the
man with the camera and the windows
offering what they could of antiquity
with all its spectacular ruins the frazzle
of marble and caryatid extending like a water
far to the east of the mountain with wings
fixtures of a mind nascent and confused
the multiple voices of the tragedians each vying
for the palm the stage-craft of obscurity

delivered in oracular incomprehension syllables
as if hewn from Egyptian basalt and the tale
the same oft repeated one identical to itself
of the god torn to bits and revived or not
revived but imagined in a hundred shapes
and tones rising from a pyramid of doubts
radiant for a moment only gathering his bits
in the vain effort to resemble his former being
a frame-up a deliquescent falsehood memory
with its nuns and nymphs in the obscure acts
meant to entertain but failing in everything
but their immense longing an aesthetic
that seems to define the soul and what
it means to flee the mortal bond the struggle
mourning and lapse and forbidden estuary
where to go on such a day how to cope
with whom to confess the inexplicable rock
weighted around the shadow as it moves
shifting from corner to corner the grief
ounces of fire inimitable reunions with space
darkness at the very center of the number
that cannot be calculated only guessed at
each hand the mummer of its own aphasia
the stumbling forth into arenas of eternity
sand in columns drifting and wavering
in an atmosphere of deictic particles a syntax
of unspoken languages and sun-spots
the how-to of a berlitz manual for the disaffiliated
you foremost sitting there in the vestibule
waiting as ever for the motor to start up
for the page to turn for the music to strike
the beginning note the unending one
which no one has ever heard

xxvi

each man in his own death
each man in his own photo
does anyone own his soul ?
left to drift across depths
water and reef and storm
bristling and there behind
that figure on the far left
that's childhood in the light
smiling and shading the eye
from the sun's fierce glare
a man with two shoulders
a thought about ice cream
or the nightly punctuation
traveling the plains of sleep
a slash in the silk curtain
a stain on the lavender sheets
memory deposited in a glass
something shimmering next
to the codicil and the feather
to wake up wondering why
the head aches shaking and
the hand and the pair of
elbows and the crease folded
in the brow and what mind
is in the fracture of space
a man is his own death nor
does he own his soul but
as a thing of recreation
a polyglot isomere afloat
in air's transparencies

a man is his own photo
his own negative becoming
a sheer column of breath
cut from rock and ether
left to error and chagrin
talking fast to the mobile
projections on the screen
imagining them to be what
is the click and the shutter
the shadow on the wall
shifting into a midnight
crimson reverie of *was*
the never of an accent
striking the syllable hard
before undergoing absence
no sound no resonance
vibrating in the lens
myth and history joined
at the waist huge stellar
stone fragments shorn
from the commencement
it is trying to learn from
the letters of nonsense
god proceeding from god
ancient vowels subtleties
that transfer light to light
outlines of impermanence
transient figurines passing
from breath to breath a
voice on the telephone
whispering infinities
when and if and but and
why merging into one

the mystical reference
characterizing the image
captured on celluloid
moving fast over time
a man is his own death
instantaneous as sand
listen from afar the waters
rushing to fill the ear
blank and ovoid immense
nowhere but in loss
wherever sky can be
in the canebrake or on
 a cart dragged by leopards
and the sun's eye blind
to all it sees and shapes
and the soul evanescent
escaping through the hole
where a finger is inserted
to keep out the dark

xvii
transients stepping on the edge of space
wherever we can be in adolescence
or in the brief transept between sun
and total blackout loss of electricity
lacking the funds to purchase salvation
a moment carved out of memory when
all things become a single unit of light
blindly sparring with our own shadows
and stopping to look at the beauties
woven into the tapestries that bear
our childhood weight the immense maze
through which we come and go oblivious of
the imminence of death at every turn
whitening in the bird-call or autumn
leaf-fall and enveloped by a sky chaste
as it is immeasurable the reaches of
parapet and turret and constellations
perceived in the noon of their passage
could we but touch their blazing trails
talk to me , Joe ! is this the deafening
by surprise of the inverted pyramids ?
what else will occur in the following minute
when finally separated we let our fingers
fold the outlines of our absence into grass
and let the porch open to the fireflies
and dancing nymphs whose voices whisper
secrets about islands and rock fragments
and seas too lush to disappear so quickly
abed with our recollection of the Map
the solar design the lunar fade the emblem

shining with the distorted glyphs of time
you sought to avenge the false epithet
assumed cartoons of enormous figures
hewn from basalt and empty lagoons
transients on the tip of the cosmos
mountains of feathers and rotting maize
a fist of stone with wings a flight of dross
antiquities of a single route to southland
the park of the dead in their quetzal suits
back and forth ping pong of the gods
laughing in their bone flutes and hair
and you the very essence one of them
gasoline and riot of a conspiracy against
convention the country club and plumbing
in the works of rectangle and even numbers
spoken through a geometry of arabesque
and native tongues you slept ! what was
the truth you inherited from the jungle wind
where was the expression to annihilate
not just the firmament but its pre-history
joking flares of a dream you couldn't share
I too slept beside that rocky precipice
overlooking the massive sea of sand
I was there when you broke the drugstore
and rifled through its lipsticks for the Drug
heave high , Joe ! you took it in deep draughts
flying like an unlocked Prometheus from
a teenage physics class into a Newtonian hell
I was the one who goaded you on into
the fourth dimension never suspecting your
false wax could not withstand the ultraviolet
shimmering that surrounded you in vapors
both crescent and immobile freezing you

in an ultrasound device impenetrable to
memory and its innocent infancy
embryonic transients on the amniotic sea
you and me , Bro'

xxviii

the hands cut off from their moorings
the little deaths subject to every day confusion
and Apollo cried amber tears though gods never cry
and then without hands and the fingers lost
in mists of grass and the mountain moved nearer
the short circuit of the stars only thirty nine weeks
and still the motionless waters and the abyss
just short of the garage in the back yard
wires and poles and a few saddened birds
not accustomed to smoke in the air could it be
the hands have nowhere to go now and memory
what little there is of it seems even more fade
the slightest gesture of the hour whose face
appears like an instantaneous mirage the fossil
and luminous insects detected scurrying on the wall
why did they have to place the body facing
north to northeast and the map showing where
the hands and the leaves rustling ever so slightly
you could never say they were voices once
you can read about it in scraps of newsprint
or pages torn from a telephone book numbers
of the asterisks still plummeting the hands maybe
up there and outlines of vague heroes shapes
of ink and cloud and the library in the middle
where on Saturdays didn't it seem just yesterday
granite and sandstone and the large windows
staring out towards the beacon big and western
as the hills that informed the horizon with a melancholy
I wonder that we can see Apollo in this daylight
his big yet planetary form and his sister too

stepping carefully across the street to avoid
the beautiful stag killed by a motorized vehicle
sometime during the late night so many things
inexplicable and oracular the hands as if shifting
of their own from the hiding places of children
who have gone missing and now wonder that
they ever had names the mysterious corners
where we wait for the traffic signals to change
what an enigma time is to have been born once
and to come out of existence and to wear red foil
and wave little banners and speak in echoes
into ears carved out of lakes and the reeds and calumets
flutes agreeing to mourn as well with Apollo
whom has he lost that he is so aggrieved ?

xxix

and the asphodel pale in the waning luster
lunar diction of phases whispered in lost dreams
a sleep olive-hued and slopes to the far west
where the slant of daylight curls in heat and growth
low and thick at first and from the other side
the high pitch of an instrument of bone or reed
the animals of burden at rest by the imagined pool
if the plants measured by the months now passed
when going back and forth to the temple ruins floor
sparse with tufts and weeds and listening for
the oracle the backwards syllables the eerie
feminine voice the intricacy of vowels darkening
and from the east a new sun a chariot bright red
wheels the axle like butter glowing in the fusion
someone high aloft waving mercurial semblance
and noon again looking for the hole the entry
underneath to the dreary realms what isn't life about
the absence of death the internal flux of emotion
and thought you'd have to go some to find
a better place a peace among the leaves and to lay
on the rock a sign a pendant a bracelet or ring
marking which point in time we are and whether
the hour will end in the circle of stone let us then
to the port to see if the ships are near if some wind
will rise and carry messages of the goddess to their
shallow ears and the drizzle of light and the force
underfoot of something we cannot discern a mystery
isn't it strange seeing in each other someone else
here button your vest hold your neck up don't
let your head to the side a prayer is something
to consider the gravel and the neat-herd by the side

pausing for the water and the invisible wings whirring
make a path for the words the secret ones who
has learned to pronounce them correctly who
can say what they mean if not the soul's reflection
the imponderable weight of their sound levitating
toward the clouds an afternoon of syllables almost
singing the ends and the inflexions the routine
here take this gem to be set on your brow and patience
the day is yet to finish its rounds the pattern of echoes
coming from the cove will we make it to the port
they say a storm is come up and the vessels
wrecked against the cliff whatever happens it is
the fates the chance of a passing deity to alarm
faint we are in the heat the circulating bluish air
sound of silk tearing and the finger daubed
in dew tracing the outline of a spirit of one just dead
how can we bear this gravity this somnolence
I want to lean against this trunk and weep
not knowing how he died so suddenly and in the
care of physicians in a distance of goldenrod and
asphodel the stem still in your hand a grayish
listening for the return of the scouts sent ahead
we lost them at forenoon and now almost twilight dusk
hush of ash and tapering lamps the remote presage
that nothing will find us but at odds with the compass
lost in brief within the single hour and hands
we hold aloft and tendencies toward madness
this solitary base where mind has no place to turn
if we could but shape the words into a constant line
into a sequence to be repeated to bring forth
the radiant One and to make of the hills a single
moment ere nightfall and the first glimmerings
in the heavens we cannot understand this enigma
being here and the sense of rain and the endless

                    XXX
at a loss which way to turn the pages of the bible
a linguistic document at best the syntax to fill
in all the blanks with arcana and doubt et cetera
stealth by floral design great open moon reddening
above the shale and slate and mist over wave
the mountain hidden within the mountain a loudness
sequestered in tiny shells echoing at the base
of the ear where myths originate and sorrow that
accompanies the immense passages of shadow and
taxed memory with details about the length of the
street the position of the original houses the burden
of leaves to keep silent during the invocation and
who was that pale with her face and inky tresses in
the background tending to the flares a reading
of the text incomplete and suddenly the nuncios
at the side gate with scrolls and sandpaper and the
mucus running from the god's nose an omen or
the furtive glances between the priestess and
her neophytes a sound of water rushing behind
the lattice and the olive trees in their Spanish get-up
how often the interruption and the fuses still to be
inserted in the walls before lighting the atrium
the mysteries catching unawares the initiates
lined up in the moorings a darkness spreading
like a frail sheet over the tops of the temples
night-birds startled and disoriented hooping
wings and a flight out of there if possible whose
voice it was whose fingers peeling the forbidden fruit
a trellis set up and stage-props a street in ancient Thebes
painted screens loosely the attire of slaves and

children introduced as a choir to sing a paean to
the deity responsible for stairs and smoke all of
this by way of a prelude to the even greater Secrets
distances between living and dead the minute hairs
in the glass the palate stuck the sweetening and offal
registries of indictment the sadness and resonance
so much crying in the eaves a victim somewhere
being led to his trial the muffled reeds and osiers
where the river used to be and the Delta oozing
out of its seven mouths and the fission in the air
as if giving birth to a new planet an asterisk or maybe
nothing more than a coffin-speech in the still noon
of the next life whorls of incense cinnamon colored
dense in the vestibule chairs scraping people as if
phantoms coming and going exchanging when possible
masks and personae the gloves that don't fit the shoes
unpaired and rhymes meant to appease the *manes*
so it goes delving into the stygian pool before dusk
the maze of dust and miasma of sputum and ire
tragedies unfolding senselessly without grammar
and as always the immense vowels the grandeur of
sleep increasing the inch of space that disappears
and the uncountable language of aphasia to regret
living having nowhere left to go and the hills slowly
unwinding their dense and enigmatic west

xxxi

black pollen the hospitals drawn in rectangles
on the slope and mists rushing swiftly down hill
to future streets the quizzical plunder at pre-dawn
justice in the leaves to speak or forever silent be
and shapes originating in dun fogs talking to
one another using pronouns until you and I
opposite the shores and battlements listing
towards Troy sent speaking you and I intent
on recognizing in each other the spent phrases
of spirits from the other world the one of rock
fragment and isolation between us the thin haze
of hesitation wasn't that a corner where you waited
and I abrupt by the plinth two fingers up wet
waiting for the shingle to fall from the roof a rain
of ashen particles could be the oracle pronouncing
in syllables borrowed from Minoan script a secret
rear worded incomprehensible as a hidden mirror
stone flutes a thickened curtain descending to
abbreviate speech acts and foiled communication
they say we cannot be that something else has
taken place where the myth begins and its consort
death and the wondrous cloths rustling in sleep
a dream with actors in outline barely shifting
across a fading painted wall to discern meaning
between characters caught in a secret dance
and stilled by a wand and the phantom god
using both left hands who has come to take one of us
away back to the origins where water has wings
darker still the depths of a face too beautiful to love
whatever inch it is we are meant to occupy and loud

the essence of the wind rushing through us dusky
lateral passions angles of suffering the iota of grief
suchness of the philosophical lid slowly opening
to release the miasma of language how can bright
ever be the sun of a newer heaven and the writing
transparent as the fingers creating it clouds absorbed
and rearranging themselves a litany of ether
the boom and distance of what we cannot remember
ourselves the souls of stuff that has materialized
and passed out of existence even as a narration
of the legend of Anima and Psyche was being recited
hard into the small and dwindling ear of Dawn
do we then *one* and the *other* cease to exist
in this long drawn out text black pollen dispersed
across galaxies that survive the death after death ?

xxxii

and I saw cutting across the rigging the form of Phoebus
high in his loud cart drawn by steeds of molten butter
the gold of ecstasy ! and should I ever turn again
to face the island of all-disappearances would I myself
be ? threats from the cloud-shaker and from under
the rippling grape colored waves shadowy substance
of the fist and trident and whistling the career of
a wind sent from the margins of space shattering
mast and ripping sail the legends of a dream tossed
aside on the other shore where I witnessed for once
the goddess rising from her split shell of borrowed light
an epiphany or a remonstrance and deep into trance
I fell reciting without knowing it the *nine names*

who came to me running uphill the languid tresses
tripartite in the sea-breeze I stifled a cry and lent
a hand to the stumbled one a surety of lace and sandalwood
from a different angle espied the shadows plotting
against stone and with skilled hands shaped from marble
the noon statuary and speaking in terms of mythical
and grand memories a nostalgia for the olden times
for the days when kings held sunset in their grasp
and in this trance I learned of Legend and the Pool
and the washing place of Nymphs and the startled deer
who had come to graze by the water's edge and what
else mattered but devotion and the spotted air mothering
the afternoon glade where my head nestled and fell
hard into the tumor of a swoon for all the world dead

against the dappled stone and thence arose the grayish
sculpture of an atmosphere dense with the deities who
confer on leaf and grass and trembling breath a soul
a dialogue between what is remembered and what has
swiftly gone from sight never to return and the abrupt cliff
the sounding surf of a sea that exists only as a Thought
a mimicry of the waters of the farthest star and turning
to read in the lawn the scattered verses of dew awoke
!

night's end his sister Phoebe the stellar vagrant her harp
making noise between the rush and wattle and the fixed
spear of eternity vibrating ever so slightly and by now her
ever vaguer shape like a cut thumbnail sailing in the sky
no longer a guide a tryst a firm decision to alter the liquid
azures the references of the tops of conifers the childhoods
implicit in the curved arm of Demeter full blown the day
out of myself the *other* I walked into the maze and swirling motes
the inexplicable city the seven gates the opened plazas
buzz and swish of a thousand beings selling and being sold
what scrap of the other eternity still clung to me what
variegated rag what senseless animal I had become

xxxiii

bodies charged with light boarding a stone boat
bound for meadows of water darkening as shadows
rent from their corpses and a voice of Alleluia far
to the right where the mountain and its ash shifts
mysteriously into the void and all falls crashing
in the sleep of glass under its own surface crystal
and basalt and a city at once appeared rearing
its turrets above the common excavations and a
room as broad as it is high in which all manner
of conveniences engines and machines that measure
heart and lung and the speed of the blood in veins
puzzling over the ancient verbs words weighted
like ore in the mouth of those who went before tight
organization of hematite and nitrous where to place
the unconscious head awaiting its translation to heaven
once on board and the ancient boatman hoary
of vision unstable and on either side the wavering
hands and banners and illegible scripts half way up
in the dense airs a smoke curling through the vitreous
container and who was the first to disembark and plant
on the fields of cold burning the claim of prerogative
it was another life another story a different city
an ambulance wailing like a kestrel above the sea
weaving and truncated forms barely surfaced and
whatever was the outcome thirty nine years in the making
human frailty defined by its own faltering limbs texts
subscriptions to a divine order the whole a volume
without margins the rush of evening stars to illumine
the saddest moment occurring in the least expected
rains and gravel and the sound of wheels disappearing

take them forever to outlast the night the escape valve
a button in the wall the green fuse the seasons blasted
all in an instant the inside and out of existence futile
and gravid efforts at speech and the tonic accent
back and forth between the same vowel and the force
the sheer velocity traversing entire space in seconds
you will say the child was but a version of that light
a form of substance and spirit combined a levity
between leaves the talking and not making sense
the hundred and one syllables divided between them
phantoms gyrating in the metaphysics of memory
one by one the marks of punctuation effaced
by a single finger of dew Dawn broken into halves
irreparable fractions never to be joined again
which was the right side and which the reverse ?
dream-speech glassy remains of echo
trailing off into

xxxiv

the warning

there is no explaining no way of getting back
and what remains is error the untrodden path
traversing the glassy surface of the noon-time sea
beneath which seethes the forensic water
have I missed the epicenter and revolved around
the mistaken mountain with its chthonic deities
each their own image of self destruction the brow
knitted in plethoric worry the thought wrangled
from a posterior nerve a pattern of lateral
conclusions a celebration of the wrong midnight
moons of faked refulgence asterisks and fists
pounding taut drum-skins in ritual display
guess who I have never been ! and in the socket
a pulse still beating a form of electricity to run
the mills of mythography the little absences
which make up half the hour and the other
half still waiting for the maternal rotation
a plangent division of sorrows a grief once
more relived and enacted on the tragic plank
drive the car over the cliff assuage the waves
below storming in their psychic brew
such is the what of common living on the *wheel*
poetry and its unwritten concussions the verb
to be rewired to its fundamental flaw a window
and the immense vowel air represents
a fix in the arm the needle piercing hard the skin
opaque and chaste imitating recollections of
the perfect summer drizzle of light and Harmony
the graceful dance of the elements at play

when grass and leaf and the formative wind
bring to mind the paradise of *others*
must we then content the self with nothing
but monotonous recitations of the verse of time
the siege of up and down and battle of reverse
toy soldiers dreaming they are but canned meat
offered to the wrathful avenger of the clouds
billowing plumes of azure smoke fattened thighs
burnt and offal spilled on the blazing altar
incense smelling salts and aromatics
that bring consciousness back to its bleak fold
why live this gifted day this extra nine
in a sequence of triple threes ? a mask worn
over another mask and sleep drained of its ink
vast panoply of persons on the verge of *knowing*
I am the *this* you are the *that* and there is no *One*
to wake is only to remember Loss and longing
a nostalgia for the islands left behind
before the chaos of make-believe and trust
only the span between thumb and forefinger
measures the distance between now and death
beautiful as they are the Nymphs wet and shining
with their promises of fireflies and pyramids
their tight embrace their multiple great hair
their bare arms glistening and their speech of bees
in them eternal solitude and somnolence
the end of rhyme and the scheme of things
be theirs and you are no more !

XXXV

the Divine Lady who is she ?
it's in the Latin dictionary !
wild sequence of interjection and vowel
macron and tonic accent fluid circumflex
diacritic and envelope of inflected words
punctuation of ether in syllabic distress
phonetic divinity serpent of light !
how do we circumvent her shadowless being
without ourselves losing shape
what is the nexus and curvature of her spine
the deliquescent knitting of her hair
as it breaks the clouds into uneven halves
mounts the disarray of sunsets she does
riding into the twilight of Romance philology
troubadours approach her castles of distance
song and infinity of archaic longing
did Zeus and Hermes require her absence ?
did Hera invoke the amended Text
to defend the godhead from her illegal syntax ?
more than a dozen irregularities and errata
per page as she takes to lyrical consequence
seas of Homeric fever and circularity
silence of Sirens in the midst of Echo !
rock and plinth and stubborn shore
yields to her buckled knee and shoulder
mounting paragraphs of early old Spanish
orange as the Cyclops' warning Eye
embolism of heat suffrage of the Naiads
drying their skins on the sun's vast trellis
grape arbor the color of night her bed

hills where no hunting is allowed and cities
large as the yearning capacities of salt !
she is the unique uppermost of space
stellar attributes burn around her voice
as she calls out to the amnesiac
nowhere to be found that saintly pilgrim
thrice holy yet desecrated by her spit
the world evolves in her spare footprint
pools where dappled deer come to drown
believing in the redundancy of water
Divine Lady leaven of lexicographers !
she could be Mount Sinai and the desert flux
Red Sea seven mouths of the Nile
wound of the migrating Cosmos
grammatical substance of the Milky Way
does her spirit imbue all the children lost and gone ?
is it she by virtue of her ordinals and cardinals
by the position of her adjectives
both remote and supernumerary
in evoking her does not *Chaos* hold sway ?
prayer and ointment of pre-Mosaic law
her raiment fluted and gracing three continents
like the Roman or Chinese empires
her histories are envisioned upside down in ivory
Etruscan letters combs and hand-held mirrors
anklets traced in Minoan linear-B
golden omegas circle her dancing arms
oratory of pebble and stardust she declaims
standing like a statue before the Alphabet
kappa lambu mu like iotas of suffused silk
come unraveling from her parted Sicilian *Lips*
yet for us does she govern a single sound
a pink sea elaborated in the inner ear

memory of all sadness in sand and cuneiform
everything we struggle to read
as we sleep in the ink of her eternal mind

xxxvi

no matter how many languages rains speak
the farthest mountain top is but a thumb away
my sweet man is dead
what's the point of this success or that
little inconsequential daily conquests fleeting
as the progress of water in a running stream
or the illusive echoes in the redundant ear of sleep
the dream of summers wrapped in grasses of wind
or leaves in their languid orient of long vowels
my sweet man is dead
what passes for a Bible and three odd psalms
a poem in virtually every dialect known
that can never be translated back into sand
what is recited at the Hour of no return when
all the noontimes stop to break bread
and who knows why but the elongated hexameter
that introduces evening and the blank verse
produced mechanically by the writing hand
and the glyphs and pictograms of the traveling seer
the histories of a broken glass and dust gathered
like a crown around consonant clusters of yearning
a thought a trembling mind a havoc of fever
reduction of all light to a single camera lens
the visible and invisible prodigies called life
breathing and being breathed by a divinity
who has never been able to climb the stairs
and of course distance which is an inch of red
measured by astronomers in the future-past
my sweet man is dead
whose idea was it to give purpose to any career

to assume that gratitude for things worn or said
and the grace and polity of a year out to sea
have any reckoning in the lunar alphabet
that goes passing like a blind finger through lawns
pronounced like afternoons in a projected fire
or that by putting on a suit and tie and walking
the fast concrete of Manhattan Island a shadow
can come back to life and sing out his lungs
the fantasy of rococo dividends and shares
my sweet man is dead
did I go to the Library to undermine the myth
and make love to the first of twenty unseen brides
to understand nothing of the *Fallacy*
and to bed go unawares each night and count
the uncontrolled vertebrae of the Text
as a method to put such idolatries to sleep
a ferry boat or a continent of wrought iron fences
the avenues numbered for their Platonic ideals
and smaller coves and nestled cities and arms
tossed out to oceans where ghosts of ivy drown
so many unfathomable and limitless the universes
and motes that turn the eye from the shape of light
the addresses lost in pockets and keys
never meant to open anything but grief
these hands and files and paper weights
these indications to shift from blue to inconsolable
minutes parked in the gravel of the stars
a motor a device to shut the empty box
where x-rays and elevators await their turn
to expose the negativity of space
yet *my sweet man is dead*
there is no more to say an entire cycle
the heat of skin giving off its allure

the steps taken backwards and the script
of hair and chaos the cosmos and its black holes
the once is gone the what is asked not to repeat
its why the talk that goes back and forth
between silences no calendars can restrain
a vacuum and a void the beauty
more sorrowful than the statues
that dot the dead-end of eternity
my sweet son is dead

xxxvii
the poles that mark either end of the globe
like the circumference and height of space
or the 20 inches that separate fire from matter
what's the difference ? a life another life
the many lives or none encompassed in the smallest
zero the ineffective One in a light
the size of a thumb-nail or the print of water
in its origins a mind could not conceive
yet we stop to pause and watch the comet's
career spin out of orbit and the lesser gods
lunching on the divine spine of ether
lose consciousness dive into the inky pool
have no way of retelling what they have forgotten
or perhaps never even saw in the single flash
the only once of eternity when birth is bright
the shining reversal of death and crib
and urn and all the phases in between
confused punctuation and vowels spread out
to comprise the never ending echo
appear and disappear in the instant of the glass
a reduct and tombstone and thumb-stretch
more infinite than the last breath expired
a revolution of sleep and stone engraved
by the tiny fingers of sorrowing memory
come back ! but never will nor can the body
illusion immersed by cloth and comb
in the uncanny deficit of time

xxxviii

unrepeatable the once beautiful it has happened
cannot ever get it back only the achingly sorrow
words with what and a spear like in the heart
piercing what good is it to have been in the light
to see hasn't it been and now gone as darkness
that moves a mystery a lunation behind it was
a door shut and if sleep too the inky depths
I will let him a cipher trying to look again
the sided rear view aspect a life drained epi-
sodes of green fusing a lush aren't you there
hallucination soda works firing clay the dark
at the end of the tongue the immense futility
downgrading the circle and where the populace
of the inferior barking regions ovoid shifts
to exclude and yearning wasn't the summer
too long over extended the sun on top of the
wind the azure blues even as eased out of its
breath the soul small effort undefined speaking
out of place and trying aloft to be a winsome
in his cart of many dialects prepared to move
as fire moves its shafts through and over the silks
a marriage of harmony to the unseen and what
is vaster and more tragic a lesson in hieroglyphs
patent erasures of meaning a syntax of sand
eroding entire planets of the heavens at a time
so terribly sorrow and the grief uncontained
every morning that I wake and set foot on the
sphere and madness of the cyclical memory
the drugstore and its hiatus the cigarette smoke
issuing from the house of Atreus and Linear-B

squiggles dots asterisks ampersands dashes and
the imperative at the end of the fuse before it
takes the whole of the other half blowing to bits
the Duomo and the Forum *have at it Man !*
minions and myrmidons the insecticides of
history pure and bungled withered on the vine
knot and bole the rotted trunk its arms raised
in lesions of air the profundities that cannot
be pronounced vowel after vowel and keep saying
over & over days of the week planetary sounds
syllables of mercury and iodine the botched x-ray
the ambulance for the last time and his own
hand over hand as sun pits its gravel beside
the quiet and its pool of echoed deer watering
each sore each festering why did we give birth
to it raising it like one of our own pigmentation
of the left eye not matching the right seeing is
not giving credit to the brief nation state he was
meant to represent numbering each blade of grass
each Etruscan tuft and tufa the merry-go-round
by the entrance to All-Saints-Day hearing as it
was intended to be tongued the Latin vulgarity
discolored and the spots mysteriously on the skin
appeared at the door asking for a handout alms
a mercy or some benediction do the gods still exist
? a fixity in the poles or the Vedic math cruelty
and precision of ordination here is the root of it
here is what causes desire and here is how it goes out
pale and obfuscated each finger in its digit and
solemnities of concrete and stone the right is upper
the down is left to the tomb of the hidden photo
aren't they smiling forever the kids caught in a
graph helium and reddening for twilight a suppose

you didn't understand and gave it to the wrong
phantom writing the thing ad nauseam classroom
chalk the distance of a black board a mountain
dust anchors of air jet streams insanity we call
it a rationale to keep going on foot after step
into the fade where there is no afterwards

xxxix

Letum Luesque, Mors Labor Tabes Dolor
                    Seneca, Oedipus
a darker country the drug and its over effects
crouching low so as to aim better the fright
unending syllable of silence shaking the thing
off its shoulder pelt and woof and hiatus cut
in half the lesser portion crimson then how
pale the cheek it represents becomes entire
write a verse magical puffs breathing the last
no other air to take in // the virginal's small
tinkling notes in the wasted atmosphere
how many words really matter two or maybe
four the number squared at the edges a summer
contained in its pronunciation fall asleep
and dream a great dream of Greeks
at their boats and the silverware shining in
the morning glint as it takes from the world
the darkened half slowly you know how it goes
don't realize you're burning until it's ash
mind and its labyrinthine contents a mirror
at each turn and thoughts up and down
cloistered idea of recovery or salvation a moot
point when there's no place left to burn
or lay the stone down where the head
sleeping the errors they call it life on earth
the dozen or so lusters that comprise being alive
a definition with many faults the easing out of
the fade and its multiple dusks setting the sun
in its sign meaning heat that comes in circles
to wake the sudden rush of inspiration uniting
vowels and consonants polyvalent echoes *High !*

Greeks by their ships wind still-dead chill to
the marrow sails useless in their dialect of unborn
air lessons recited mistakes in punctuation era
of shells and smaller figures detritus floating back
and forth on the mucus colored tide will it ever be
able to move into a lunar period a phrase at
a time a denunciation of Nemesis and what
it stands for bodies just lying there multiple
freighted in opaque sand an inchoate twilight
hovering dense palpable humid presences
things that cannot be felt who fled downwards
taking with them scraps of meat disembodied
fates determined by lottery for an early end
bells tolling sirens eerie note inaudible at first
who will follow them into unredeemable depth
who will mark differences between aorist and
preterit and the perfectly completed

and I saw on the shelf still glowing the *spirit*
though none were there who could touch it
and if we are *down* and the god is no longer within
what is the sign the hand the index finger the grass
what leaf exactly blown in the right direction
will continue to speak ?

a disk a quoit a whizzing in the ear
wave over wave the reflection of a
branch dipped
the tall pine
felled to
sail

xl

tiny diameters spools things still whirring
fever clinging to the spine and the echoes
of names of what was once felt the senses
how many of them in meadow or pool
reflections drawn from dissolved memories
set the body in place worship the breath gone
fissures in air cracks in evolving space
heavens in the faint traces of the x-ray
dynamics of sheets pulled back seas roiling
under the bed's relaxed springs pale
and even more fade the increased inch of wall
the stair at the end of darkness the underside
of evening shifts and sound of gravel a god
unsure of direction hesitates before Poof !
disappearing again into his alter ego *sleep*
which is the potter's field and which the clay-pit
footsteps styles of noise in nocturnal increments
a crypt and its valence the size of a thumb
pointing east by northeast toward the rock
fragmented into quarters inscribed crushed
an envelope that contains all the remnants
hair and oil-tin and bicycle chain caught
on the pant-leg of infinity something shifting
in the captured skin now a dissected thought
remembrance of afternoons spent in pure heat
vision of the *other* in its absence and listening
for the paper to bend its own page of gravity
sighs and relentless silences in reaction
to the door and what is behind it a past
of lost possibilities toys and dust embolisms

the last hour of chaos! what is the occurrence
in the telephone or the photograph clipped
in its marginless distance and the children
frozen in chiaroscuro recognizing the *once*
of that moment the vowel and the lens and
how everything collapsed back on the syllable
that no one has ever been able to pronounce
a library of uncatalogued emotions a sadness
to impart shapes to the final summer if
and only if it had ever been the excursion
to the mountain the prayers in mist and cloud
fusion of orient to the mantra of déjà-vu
what else has ever mattered but learning
to give it up birthright and alphabet and
tendencies toward depths toward the unkenned
a hand multiplying itself in defiance of speech
to beckon and hail and warn the angel amiss
in the harrowing architecture of breath
wings bleeding light and grief

xli

and they declared what they thought it to be
the end of a life and said so this is it
lamps lowered and they laid the body
shifting as little as possible of its gravity
and went about sweeping the floorboards
and washing the rugs and with a certain decorum
waited for the ones who would claim it
in their full grief oblivious of the rains
and so neither inside or out did there seem
to be any difference in the material world
and there was talk about the script
and the correct pronunciation of vowels
and laying by its side the shining objects
that most befitted memory of days on earth
being careful to make as little noise as possible
lest the deities of the inferior world aroused
should appear and stake an early claim
outside the large opaque window a downpour
making the sound of an immense waterfall
and the chief physician came to console
taking the surgical gloves off his hands
wiping his eyeglasses uncomfortable for the hour
the wall-clock being the sole thing sounding
its tiny echoes reverberating infinitely
in the ear a presupposition of the vanities
of the stopwatch or the links of small gold
the minute hand chasing the instant keeper
as if anything of that mattered and space
itself reduced to such dimensions as an ant
can traverse in a moment's notice

difficult as the situation was and for those
who guard the doors against darkness
and the night-clerks alert to any brightness
of color outside the regulated scheme
sitting at attention in a mythological gravel
imagining the great vehicles of the gods
passing back and forth noiselessly through
the substantial walls of the present world
carefree and careless of the sorrowing at hand
for a brief second everything came to a stop
gone the memory of the park swing
and the greenery effervescent of a July afternoon
a swimming hole or a perch high above
the canyons of salvation and the many and the
few who cling to names and syllables
declared it to be over with and lifted luggage
and unused bedclothes and sheets and
the yellowing mystery hanging in the air
the shape of silence in its last contours
murmurs of ink and distance going out
nothing left to be defined the tears
immense as dew and in the corner
the guy who invented music bursts
out weeping

xlii

so forth and the rest a looming cloud a
darkness before midday threatening
the body as it goes through its daily maze
a choice of music or bullets a phrase
designed to enlighten but only depresses
look at the footnotes try to figure out
which one got it and who survived
the mere possibility of a call from beyond
so much intensity and beautiful letters
like wings going aloft a phase at a time
if you can read at the bottom in fine print
a typology of sorrow a distinct version
angelic and gilded edges a fringe fraying
at the touch a lexicon of eastern Latin
some three miles to the left of Hellespont
a diction in hills and twilight a dun
fading ineffably in this cemetery of words
I don't know why I keep on living do you ?
tales and fictions and lengthy lies the
ambulance has come with the mail and
the heights of glyphs the cribbed passages
the bad translations and legendary sums
add up to nothing the failed lunation
the miles of tongue and abject sound
echoes of a refrigerated past a spoonful
haunted the ghosts who certainly round
the sleeping bends a chromatic seizure
the harrowingly gorgeous swirls skirts
slipping by the inflected forms of echo
and night the always with its tunnels

of abstract art heaps of lead painted
dusk at the end of a trial anonymous
if a face and its hands the docile ear of
symphonic accompaniment have at it
the crossroads puzzling and deserted
at this hour of the evening scary shapes
come forth and if I can't go on another
day can you ? capsized thimbles of water
the pool the deer come to drink and die
the buddhas at least forty identical
to one another and the round dance of
moons epileptic in nature swarming red
vertigo as a definition of love the vowel
at the end of each exclamation while
I undress the syntax of its structure a
sky an ability to return gold to its sunset
enabling the hearse of mythology to move
lumbering through the defiles an end
to the beginning of death the receipt
for an unfinished book pages of blank
issues the Nymph and her drowned
iotas thunder and verbatim of absence
my fingers the number of leaves left
to count who are still talking fainter
than pale the ever fade of

xliii

emptiness defined the remainder of my turn
neither the globe above shining like mercury
nor what passes for earth below shifts and turns
illogic of calendar pages dotted with unknown
sequences of sleep and fits of waking in the dark
snatches of light pursed cylinders pages torn
from the book of pyramids the inverted dance
of memory traveling its belt-line highways
through a renaissance of glimpses and mosaics
in a dizzy kaleidoscope none of which can return
loss to its former elegance a puzzle or an orient
littered with grassy tufts and the sudden mountain
reared like an extension of night into heights
darkening and denser than thunder-cloud fabric
from which there is no precise way out no route
through the middle sea of metaphysics no verger
leaning westerly in fond remembrance of greenswards
did I lay the stone there once and carve glyphs
indicating steps to take clearing the path for a life
that was not meant to be and pausing at hills or
framing between thumb and jib the distances
possible before exhausted each possibility simply
fades way and perplexed at a dusky crossroads
I learn to count my dead the now many who have
passed out of the reflecting glass into somewhere
that the poem cannot console the ineffable
diction of oblivion with its immense unshaped vowels
echoing the portions of sorrow the airs and winds and
flutes driving through the leaves like voices no ear
can catch the thinner threads and threnodies the

absolute of absence and sand combined that exist
on the edge of an undefined space of a corollary
of masks and persons last seen moving weightless
from the world of matter and myth into the ether
no hand of gravity no finger of pointless clocks
nothing but the increment of grief in each shoulder
the rain that scours a single rock for days on end
the once and only ending to the graph of breath
beautiful for an instant only colored like the dew
on the expanse of lateral worlds elisions and wounds
in the origins of time a saddle-backed ridge of air
nothing to cling nowhere to hold the immense inks
billowing out of the vacuum at the bottom of water
only this emptiness that creates nothing more than
thoughts that vanish unexpressed never heard

xliv

and another thing I have to say
being gone and back from the ruins of Taormina
in the rain and memory incised here and there
in archaic rock and stone graffiti in the air
intaglios and inchoate sea buffering wild shore
lisping summer runes in the vatic atmosphere
was here the ideal realm designed and shadows
crawling on the walls depicting maenads
swarming Aetna's perilous purple slopes
a lad I was then smart-eyed mythographer
unconscious as the insect that traverses ears
of wheat in a yellow daze to perforate the future
I too intuiting each legendary mile each echo
coming back from half-translated bucolics
pastorals evoking idioms of marjoram and marigold
narcissus and hyacinth blending transparent hues
in the sun's enormous splash of daylight a loss
before its time a longing to sow stardrift
in the furrows of the mind's uncreated epic
a yearning and the source of grief sorrowing
in the undesignated winds whipping the canvas
and rope of an imaginary fleet at Siracusa's knee
had I but stopped to listen to each leaf bleed
its separate voice its trellis and vine of tragedy
would my life's career have been altered a threnody
instead of a surrealistic paean to the goddess who
governs hemline and anklet a jangling of silver
in the broken sleep of one who has learned
too late the buckled spine of unformed oracles
words like mazes and syllables snapped like twigs

underfoot in the trance-like tarantella a man
is forced to dance on the eve of what he most fears
death and its gorgeous understudy casting
her miles of inky hair to unwed Zephyrus
alphabets of salt and remorse a brow swept
away by the endlessness of Heraclitean ether
and another thing I have to say
going through empty Sicilian hotel rooms
embroidering remembrance of the colossal ruin
with the delicate consonants left by the Soul
in its furtive but sudden ascent into the void
is and nothing more

xlv

archaeology of the archaic both glyph and ant
midges wings and hill-ridge toxic deities and hummingbird
black eye-liner white peplos opened at the middle delta
and midstream shipwreck and mountain mysteries
trident and numen and sisters-three the wheel and
necessity the sorrowing inch the first and last day
one and tomb and five and the fatal summer
otherwise the center is not the solid whole
the less and its telling grass and narcotic spoons
and sky they fill and verging on miasma the echo
of chaos where it begins beside water and its reflection
men like planets plummeting and women in the first
of twenty portals and twins and death the nymphs unwind
punctuation and grammar of unhewn marble
steps carved at the half-way mark and zones worn
around the waist and bees in swarms of blindness
like nights of stone like rock and silver orgies
temples dedicated to Ruin and loudness of sapphire
and reunions of the soul with its cancer and ebb and
ire and tide and reflux of sand the missing unit at the head
the column without origin the arms of bric-a-brac
discovery of iron and rust sections of air mutilated for
their price and beauty in its scaffolding above the sphinx
crossroads and clouds darkening at the source where
ink takes shape and nightly birds that cry and grieving
visit dreams in the size of vowels and aphasia to speak
of fates and phantoms without sutures and simulacra
of Helen repeated in the cast of characters pronunciation
and syllable of the oracle cave and shadow field of ore
yellow versus hyacinth drowning on the other shore

words that have no lexicon and prefix and blackness
seized by passion at the helm governors of riot
set out to noon and branded cattle of the sun and
twilights beneath a legging of pure china silk
an end to the opaque and luminous couplets
recited into the Dionysian Ear if something else
resounds and touch of alpha beside the wrecked circumflex
how will it read who will describe the text what classroom
destroyed by its own written chalk the flame and
the eagle the isolated penumbra of the Furies
high and aloft and the chastened thumb that weeps
how else explain the ineffable the root of all human
misery the desire and its portent and ambrosia
where Chronos drifts a vast a lost a singular epithet
twice and thrice alive and followed by Nemesis
into the numberless accent of the stars

xlvi

tragedy geminated consonant followed by full moon
nothing less than the reddened circumflex rising
over unbidden seas that divide two from its half
no need to count the rain the simulated era of numbers
is over and the time of stammering hands is nigh
the whole cannot be contained by a small vowel
the legend of the extended shadow and its stone
the possessed mouth of the princess of Arabia
and her double pacing in stiletto heel shoes
how much in the pharmacopeia of madness can
be settled by the whitening bread loaf and its knife
dawn with its mismatched horses running amok
all bright and shiny as the forged inks of India
the sands of the rivers run dry in their dialect
and issuing mysteriously from a bed of narcissi
the articulation of fever the still-born consonant
etching the sky before its curtain of burning isolation
wherever there is a cup to bear and a potion stirs
and lips that seal the ivory syllable of love in disdain
the hardening core of darkness deep within the eye
worn like a sleeve of mercury in the fascination
that day will not break this noon nor whiplash and
detritus the ruins encumber with the faded lava
running from the pores of a sleeping statue placed
on its side beside the quotient of breath allowed
the hour in its contest with rock to overcome
why is it then that words cannot express this fate
this perilous slope that winds up in a distant cove
that ships and slaves and migrating waterfowl
decked out like alphabets of crimson gore the heavens

flail and bring down gods to their knees and
silver amulets and tears in flagons and priceless
jewelry louder than the emerald inlet of Hermione
and crushed under the roving Wheel a small numen's
finger of woven grass and woof and web and welkin
the tinderbox unite and fuses of springtime verdure
the bedside do adorn and fearing to crash in the ear
the precious spotted roe and deer to Artemis rush
wildly in the speed of a smoking turf and settle
beta and omicron next to the temple's fallen gate
here it was the dagger struck and high above the sound
of brass the spear that could not stop and the inch
of fabric imitating flesh was rent in a terrific echo
aphasia of the dozen tongues and by shoulders borne aloft
to the Olympian symbol that stands for leaves deep
green to be chewed until the mind can take no more
and it is precisely here as well that you and I , yes
little comfort find in the image of one whose soul
has been elevated to the vast but missing light
how masterful the unwritten score the text of dots
and stops and lingering sobs vanishing like chaos
in the marginless surf of time

xlvii

the repetitions the difficulties repeated the days
without end that are in fact at an end this dawn
of expurgated light of nocturnal absences of music
for moon and fiddle and insects too craven to face
a world as minuscule as the shard of glass stuck
in the pacing foot and a flood of oil and cavities
where the ends of words go when they can no longer
be pronounced the echoing silences of thoughts
of adumbrations of mind of the opaque silhouettes
shifting in the dappled hues of sleep before waking
a cry of solitude and isolation a worm growing
where the center used to be and dark matter with
its perspectives of grief and ownership without hands
longing as the sole ontological unit the varying
shades of distance and cliff and hanging in mid-air
the candle still burning like a warning about history
the relentless ages miswritten in pamphlets half
destroyed by the lamp and from behind sealed paper
instructions for dying and capsizing and hesitating
round and round the same hour goes in a circularity
of heat and remission of sins and for every alpha
that strikes its puzzling note an omicron loses weight
sand drifts are great by the dampened window and
a room that was not here yesterday manifests large
and dimensionless with bare walls and a fluorescence
that does not diminish and there are voices with
long extended vowels and combs and waxen *things*
it is for sorrow that these minutes pass surrendering
their emptiness to the page awaiting illumination
frozen digits numerals of disorder a chaos of air

constructs of memory resembling stairways of
smoke repeated ad infinitum that lead nowhere
but to the singular dream of *being* with its mistakes
of being born of growing to a certain size before
falling ill and losing consciousness and retaining
of the shadow its interrupted speech patterns its
hiatus of water suspended in a marble thimble
the so many occlusions and secret ciphers x-rays
situations of doubt and sepsis and the frequencies
of doorways and corridors and repetitions et cetera
nausea of having to wait for the inexplicable to be
reiterated on small crumpled sheets of drug-store
because it is the *not-knowing* that is the envelope
incoherence of shorn hair and blades of grass lining
the slender crooked passageway that leads to disbelief
notes scribbled on the inside of the left ear and a shout
loud as the cloud shaped like the instep of Artemis
that appears and disappears in the alternating eye
so many the immense fabrications of imagination and
space and time and the bullet of reverie that strikes
again and again in the final childhood of illusion
a life a life to be that was now gone forever

xlviii
island of white splendor
blankets of white clouds sifting
through skies of emerald and pearl
sleeping marble of white statues at midday
memory and dim recall of the seas
mist over wave wave over shadow adrift
air in its complex structure of longing
cut through by keen winds divine breaths
have lived too long it says on the margin
where atmosphere darkens and earth's
smaller states dissolve slowly in
the tacit governance of the mountain
goddesses of necessity and angst converge
at the still point of diminishing echoes
leaving behind only a single extended vowel
the shape of distance the bay of loss
what is being erased if not evidence
of the summer when life in all its array
spread brightness the ineffable day of
bee and hummingbird and talking leaf
underfoot the grass and ant-hill and
surface of mind taking in all its imagery
whiter still the immense and invisible syntax
of the child in his heroic size of ink
and paper folding and unfolding
in the improbable flight of hands
moving aloft toward the frayed moons
of prediction and fate reddening then
turning pale the faded twilight
and the island of white splendor gone ?

and the blankets of white clouds sifting
through skies of emerald and pearl
now shredded tufts of stained bedding
midday and the sleeping marble
and the statues that will not wake again
eyeless staring into the unwritten void
exercise of language in its final shift
distribution of echo in the mountain
dissolution of mountain in its shade
and the siren buried in the ear
all this the goddess of cremation
with great emotion in her embrace
sets high on balconies of smoke
and disappears in a commotion
of infinitely white silence

xlix

host of flows one over nine night's
adze on edge will one of them ever get
it ? flues and raffled rays of sunlight
at this bower of the flight and sum of
all tides the great crippled Zeus with
his parley of egrets and swans the dipped
trench filling mossy overload the rill
of time in a single drip through space
language cut through by doubled water
the sword of glistening perforation
swashing index finger at the knuckle a
bone blast freeze hurts so much the small
clip stuck in the cavity and emergent
swells roiling miniature seas troubled
by the mind that conceived theses quarts
distributed unevenly over the hemispheres
that dazzling fire the chaos of light as
even the splendor grays at the margins
please as to suffer the kinder bruises
a wanton but pale fray into dream-scans
x-ray and burst thermometer the fever
was so mythical the lace so friable the
accent on the tripled omega and to sound
the way it ended as sad an echo as ever
the event was rainy an afternoon in the
quad the professors jiving Sanskrit over
their numinous tablets of soma to swallow
or not the result in neon overlay how many
had still to analyze the speeches in marble
the statuary in odes and hemline bleeding

like flashlights in the ovarian conduit
how could anyone have predicted fate
to be so immutable so visceral I was in
the hall howling and darker still the ones
on stilts with their enormous vowels barely
held like weights on their shoulders hands
stuttering like crazy trying to reconstruct
memory of that late hour waiting for
the jet to land on that small roof a drugged
brother in tattered weaving a shirt through
his brain thinking it was a moth a flame
to approach and littered in old Minoan
dialect scripts handled cruelly the part
played by Cassandra on the raving steps
it was for my lost one the little chance
he had visiting in so few days the twenty
and one entrances to hell and the gasoline
and his hair and the twilight adumbrating
so beautiful on the hills hiding their gold
in trace and gesture to minimalize down-
loading the photo in its carbon phases
each of the figures washed in a lamp
of pale contours behind them a mountain
the suggestion that this was earth its
rumbling tectonic plates its nocturnes
were they but what the dreams meant
remembering so sweetly the longing
and the Wheel lifted ready to make
its final turn over each of the syllables
articulated by the masks now fading
the origin of the world it was called

1

years of yearning the small effects
of death before its time antiquity
of things that grow with distance
hemline and stitching of the stars
even the vaguest in their parallels
to fates on earth tiny gemstones
coruscating in the invisible hand
that sorts vowels from consonants
such as language is abrupt and often
senseless inky soundings eerie phrases
joined to the tip of each finger words
oracular and mysterious spelling out
a system of air of nebulae of asteroids
seizures of the brain in extreme light
the foil and fable of something gone
wrong an infancy in reverse clothes
that never fit arm-braces extended
shoes meant to walk sideways into time
if we could but understand the why
of each dot each missed punctuation
of the lessons in red and silver and agate
on the chalkboard the absences aching
in tone and accent flights of reverie
will this ever be explained the doodling
on the prescription paper the circumflex
which only the pharmacist can read
what were they trying to say the voices
torn from the leaves outside the window
gardens of archaic stone and water
stepping over the dead lotus and fade

image of faces in the pool being drained
of its lamp the sutures that appeared
overnight and the scrabble and tongue
eyes and flutes and secret appendages
uselessly attached to the wrong dream
the one about the bicycle on the hill
glowing with its fantastic three wheels
how will the other side of the slope
increase its inch and whether the rope
tied around the blood is ever tight enough
a different entrance procures silence
and the music of an alphabet of harps
listening closely the ear will apprehend
that the sea sounds different on Wednesdays
the day of miscalculations and sorrow
not realizing what that desperate glance
really signifies the winch and the wheel
the unseen instruments preparing to
take the soul from its dumb show
so much recalled and forgotten
in the flicker of ash
as it ascends
unknown

li
given the inclination to die
not knowing why you lived and
the bunches of rain like fists
troubling the air in dark knots
fighting pounding sighing winds
downpour sent by almighty Zeus
from his purple pavilion of clouds
childish figures intaglios halved
by an otherworldly light you ask
me if this isn't some kind of joke
asterisms and perfumes wafting
back to sleep to dream inconsequential
write another line of the ineffable
wake up in fits and starts at
the window the ceaseless early
winter tempest chills of a tale
told once too many the gods playing
cards at a three-legged table
laughter like hollow cataracts
pouring down the mountain-side
precious little to hope for when
so many already departed and
wan shapes flitting in the mist
distances and torpors legends
of a music distaff or sailing ships
sirens swimming in nectar or
ambrosia ruffians and Dravidian
brigands waylaying travelers
daring the southern steppes in
search of a mantra a magic potion

a syllable correctly pronounced
that might bring some truth
to the experiences of ennui and
unfulfilled promise hello you say
speaking to the wharf in the mirror
where they are unloading statues
resembling figures of myth with
heads snapped off shattered arms
but still speaking in sonnet forms
wildly disparate in their assonance
and meter the silence ensuing
captures the rain in small cups
ivory and porcelain and the jagged
edges of the sky still roaring away
siestas are impossible and longing
and inveterate sadness unable to
cope with the day's dwindling hours
whether to stare at a moving screen
or simply in remorse of breath
and peculiarities of language and
trope spell out the remote histories
of silk and sand caravanserais
loaded with archaic literatures
written in glyphs and pictograms
homophones of the sun replicas
of moon-sounds jabbering in
the ear what can you make of it
the rain the thunder of immense
hammers thongs and tongs and
brilliant sparks for a moment as
if all the cosmos had just broken
into its literal hemispheres
an echo at a time

lii

"El humo a la llama, la llama a la brasa, la brasa
al leño, el leño al árbol, el árbol a la tierra, la
tierra al sueño."
Miguel Ángel Asturias, Hombres de maíz"

all the air shaking and the shadow of air
like a wave over vanishing light the depths
what remains of the human what echoes
in the ear of the mind passing as it does
from the field is the rustling sound of grass
breaking through soil of speech distantly
rising from the House-Underneath a voice
asking for something back whether the shape
of hands or the simple device that lets sleep
enter the slightest leaf the trembling tender
color now become dormant and if I told you
none of this matters that I have been to
the domain of Persephone white haunts
illusory lamps flickering in a twilight
of language and have spoken even with
the phantom Helen and seen Cassandra
on a rave with cigarette in either hand and
smoking on her step of incomplete ascension
syllables of the manicomio and bedlam and
to them I addressed the red soliloquy of
amnesiacs who are left to search for names
within the confines of the wandering Thought
to have back my son to recall my brother from
the wreckage and ravages of disease and time
to you also I bring to mind the errant isles

the soporific volcano of existence the ire and
flute of Apollo who commands the sun but
cannot control it to have at the tree-of-life and
pull at its roots and waste the night in vain
spoil of stars and reverie ghosted absences
sorrowing branches sawed off after midnight
and if I told you that as often as I have visited
Pluto's mansion and tarried there conversing
no less a figure than Agamemnon in his gold
mask the person of rock and fiber the illustrious
gave me no portion of the darkness stood
his ground deader than the most I have ever
known and forming immense vowels in spite
but saying nothing that I could have understood
listening for an oracle in the dry well outside
the entry to the After-Life and so much else
a pattern of deceit and planetary flight of
days stricken from the calendar and likened
to the souls in purgatory and sulfurous moments
I spent beside the jostling ship of spirits
the maimed blinded and deaf to reason the ones
among them I searched and pleaded and
even offered bottles of the coldest white wines
the noontime of descent and the cavernous
replies from within solid stone and the Hecate
herself the beautiful and awful whose shuddering
illuminations of moon eliminate all hope
what does it care the long lost days revolving
on a spindle high held in the fist of the Parcae
ululations and tremblings and sotto voce
dread how else can I explain to you the other
side of things the darting snares of animae
when none that I asked for none that I almost

recognized it was not *Max* it was not *Joe*
feverish striations of air in columns thick and
quivering casting no direction and oceans
immense and rushing with silence the eternal
and always the bodies of memories pale
like the fading and illusory western hills
indistinct as afternoons of a cancelled summer
smoke to flame flame to ember ember to wood
wood to tree tree to earth earth to dream

liii

where have they gone the half-letters
the unfettered locks of hair the frail leaves
left to fly float and slowly fall to dense earth
the darkened where light drains and noon
when statues are most alive and yearning
to talk to tell of what they have seen and
heard in the blind journey from rock
to tremulous air the bright unfastened
realm of wind voices and echoes in the ear
what have they done with the fingers and grass
the unwinding of a braid of thought
beside the flowering tree or water running under
the canopy of sunlight toward its dark source
puzzles of the hour imaginations like drizzle
on the sleeping shadow riddles and enigmas
the unkenned word issuing from nowhere
suddenly become a poem or a song unfinished
memories never identical fading
the outline of a body moving of its own
over a field vivid with a text of flowers
lengthy syntax borne of rock and surf
meters high above the world's pellucid acre

souls not yet born or just released
from the coil hover trying to recall *the* why
and beasts lumbering in a dream of wagons
and treks through mountains and lakes
take on semblances filmy and wet of persons
mythiform and with arms upraised and incense
in wreathes around their heads and another

larger longer sequence of syllables like
gourd rattles or lamentations of Zephyrus
weaving through the ornamental ivy of the hill
minds in repose flocks of exquisite metaphor
cloud formations studding the vacancies of sky
soon it will be the day after the funeral and
a new language spackled with consonant clusters
deformations of stops and moon-dots
the ear will not apprehend the tongue unable to
repeat uttering a hobson-jobson of appeals
in suppliant vowels criss-crossing the Hour
distance itself at a standstill in a horizon of
glyphs that cannot be recombined into words
longing and the infirmity of breath alike
how can it ever come back the spent flame ?
left behind the errant *self* the persona
bereft of characteristics a blank oval facing
the enormous cliff-side of space rising
with its novels and edicts of asterisms and
shifting spectra the beginning and end
of the idea of *being* half-letters frail
narcissi and anemones of the field
lying in the hush of unending sleep

liv
"Mundum revelli sedibus totum suis
ipsosque rupto crederes caelo deos
decidere et atrum rebus induci chaos"
          Seneca, Agamemnon, 485-487

took flight about an hour before midnight
worlds in a thumbnail verbs kept irregular
nothing sorted out baggage remained opened
bed and plume and bath and warmth seeping
out sheets knotted disarray of visibility magnet
and suture and left hand inoperable the switch
and glass small trickles staining walls
floorboards and the air smudged with a faint
breath tracing shape of a leaf the disguises
able to move an inch or so into the ionosphere
key and fling and baffled heat in circular
irreparability like gods too perfect in their
geometries to care wherever earth gapes and
sections of ocean too winding like a serpent
around the mountain lidless eyes staring into
scraps of paper floating in search of a script
pharmaceutical levers waning stairways
a whole instead of a half the sky isolated
in its disunion from space the idea of motion
which is verbiage sorrowing finger and knuckle
a single bone rattling to be heard by nurses
waking still speaking in a dream Tagalog
shifts of river currents imminent tremors
ready to remove the island from its mooring
to ask what are the ninety on the meter or

when does it gravitate to the hundred and four
so difficult to interpret the hundred and thirty
without sunshine the sea levels rise gradually
from the myth of stasis and the beached whales
dozens mysteriously washed up does one recall
toy afternoons on pink sands and fragility
something swift could come along and distances
barking and melancholy the partitions between
beds in the same room coughing that irrupts on
the fringes of grief who is no longer there where
expected the side-railings the multilevered pillow
those things that protect the feet from sores
developing after days of inhibition and promises
to send out for salvation and tonic despite
sidelong glances the knowing hemlines the needle
prepared to take but not to give back the blood
maps of serial illnesses patients hooded figures
night-crawlers with flashlights looking for serum
took off at the right time before the clock could
hold back the hour and recidivism be enacted
hollows and fuses and *Ping !* metabolic conclusions
charted in thin crimson lines at the top of
the machine that invents breath thirty times a
minute an arm of fog that holds out for more
door-knockings futility of the dinner bell and
what's more the lock on the elevator so no
one can go up or down // intravenous paradise
emptiness and confusion of the paratactic zero
cannot identify what comes after number forty-nine
seraphic versions of the vowel that divides *now*
from the immense wasteland of tomorrow
wave beneath and wave above the tent of light
chaos that filters and absorbs the universe

lv

life has become too difficult
breathing in short fits and starts
the barking in the ears a lost landscape
heart and pulse out of line imagining
the wastes above and below the heavens
the plural of darkness revolving in the number
that lies hidden in the Mystical Union
ages from the beginning of light the first
and second hours of space that emerge
flowering billowing with great and
erratic punctuations asterisks and
plumage of quotation marks in dissolution
a land beyond the land where they bury
the poets who never made it
to their publication party an effervescence
of platitude and reverie *that could have been me*
the world is a jostling hole a fierce
contest of taxi-rides and perilous beaches
sunsets behind a rock that harbors
night eternal and the grief of a day just spent
never knowing why or how
the unlimited hands that reach out
only to find that nothing is within grasp
and the as ever notion of *mind !*
yet life has become too *too* difficult
a reason just one more to jettison
the impulse to wake again and thrive
routine and its penciled mannequins
at the foot of the bed salute the erstwhile *you*
while invisible machines graph the peninsula

known as isolation its fever and pitch
and sulfur with irreverent appeals
to the deities whose delight is to destroy
the common myth of immortality
incumbent upon the written text that
appears and disappears beneath the sheets
palpitations and hours on end of sad remembrance
the child who was and never will be again
or the summer wrapped in cellophane
and the shouts and cries of the circus
on the edge of town where morticians
and clowns surprise the crowds
with acts of trapeze and free-flight falls
without a net to land in Pluto's realm
am I a Dante without sleeves
a being with half a self who wanders
from gyre to gyre in perplexity ?
this life this contentious drumroll
these lamps that shine on and off
like mercury draining through a sieve
what's to know about the other world
about the manuscript rolled in a bottle
what's to understand of the second coming
or the reincarnation of the missing page
alive or not the minutes tick off
to look and never see what's straight ahead
the Beatrice and her antinomy
immense fogs and cliffs and verses
of the last and forever epic lost

EPILOLGUE

immensity of the tragedy ink beyond measure
flowing over Greek who are writing the absences
the difficulties the losses when letters are not fit
cannot ascribe to the lesser deities nor who first
arcane emitted the sounds echoes and solutions
over rock and matter the eloquence and singing
voiceless meters quatrains vaster than hexameters
seas brought to the sky and heavens immersed in
tempests greater yet either nostalgia or home-coming
their ships and shafts and poles and masts shattered
winds at war with winds and air itself reduced to
a knot singularity of blown through a canopy of
clouds like ire and thunders and the vessels lost
forever over the edges of the Ptolemaic earth
square root of the verb that leads to paradise and
suns one hundred and one of them blazing together
to end war and misery and the breathless soul of
one floundering on a reef and travesties his memory
shot the legend of myths of ego and self and persons
masquerading as History wherever rumor presides
and doubt the surfeit of gain and still aimless mortals
reckoning an abacus and a thumb and sighting high
the precipices of invisible planets houses of the Zodiac
fates and triple-goddesses and dust in vestiges of light
whoever and whatever this all means alphanumeric
decibels the rate of increased of incrementation of
the ineffable and indescribable *let me tell you* and
et cetera fogged and jammed in the ear-wave sleeping
dross and quintessence being written and erased

one at a time until the only one left is the flagstone that
lists beside Zero shadow and bulwark of emptiness
how isn't that sad ? why doesn't it recommence ? why
should the ending already be at birth the small digit
turning around itself in the enormous playfield of thought
rigid waistline tight and orphic consonants fixtures
like lamps burning just above mind's puny surface
but always comes down to one thing *death* you know
lying there in its oils and ribbons and sublime pomp
a little tattered at the seams but overwhelming nevertheless
and it comes to grieve and the swamps and promissory
notes and the musicality of leaves mourning summer
so many indications events experiences half-recalled
yes and no please don't and the wall which completes
the street and the hedges lined up fragrant lilac and bay
beneath them the almost visible realm of Pluto the soils
mixed as ever with Remains and watered and prayed
setting up altars and incense bins the fettered everyday
weather deconstructed memory the brain a hive of
mewing withering transactions a faint the febrile cast
pale and the fade the evanescent the epitaph of sleep

12-08-18